Rockin' in the Spirit of

Love

SHELLEY STRAND

ISBN 979-8-88540-669-7 (paperback)
ISBN 979-8-88540-670-3 (digital)

Christian Faith Publishing
832 Park Avenue
Meadville, PA 16335
www.christianfaithpublishing.com

Printed in the United States of America

CONTENTS

PREFACE

I was asked by Pastor Garth Roberts to write about the life of his wife, Margaret. I am not an author of novels and wasn't sure of how to get her story off the ground, and the same went for starting each chapter.

I chose to write clear and simplified; in other words, my written expression of language might remind you of the early to mid-1900s, which I felt was fitting. I write poetry and Christian songs; however, this novel of Margaret turned out to be my best experience of all my writing, thanks to God for bringing me into her life seventeen years ago up until her passing on January 16, 2020.

Her story supplies the reader with facts and illustrations. The poems I wrote reflect her experiences in at least a few different personal ways to connect her life to the book in an honest and loving way; they are an extension to elaborate on her life and character. The scenes played out in the chapters will hopefully have the reader laughing and satisfied with the shaping of the road in life that God walked her down. She lived out Scripture which needed to be added as a part of decorating her journey in her Christian work and family life and to give God glory.

The novel is designed to create lifelike memories of Margaret, for those who didn't know her and those who barely knew her. Those who knew her best and loved her most, I designed it to add living joy to their lives. Hopefully that's the case.

Through prayer, I asked Jesus to take me in and out of the chapters, to walk me through the information from their long-lived personal letters, to help me use my knowledge and perception of her effectively, as well as conduct interviews with Garth and daughter, Esther, for making notes. Included were massive amounts of text messages with Garth and picture albums with timelines. I needed the Lord's direction every page of the way.

I wanted her novel to be full of true adventure with some fictitious moments. I say fictitious because no one knows every thought or every single experience Margaret may have had, therefore letting me add flashes of color along the way. The book is a bit like *Little House on the Prairie*, teaming with proper humor, interesting scenery and uncomplicated real characters. I believe it will read clear and colorful!

Last of all, I wanted this book to put the light on the godly example of her marriage and ministries. I apologize to family if I left out important moments that I wasn't aware of. The best proofreaders will be them.

ACKNOWLEDGMENTS

Thank you.

I first thank Jesus for taking me through Margaret's life in the way I believe He wanted it written. By working with my level of ability, which is not of the degree of excellent authorship, He directed and used me to tell others about what He can do with one life in bringing many to His glory.

I thank Aila Strand, my granddaughter, for a group of useful words for the book that she thought upon first.

I thank John Strand, my son, for helping me think up an important title for Margaret's book. God was involved again.

I thank Darryl, my husband, for helping to get the book in arrangement such as font size and cover page details that I needed for the final drafting.

I thank Margaret for her love and her Christian example of living like the Bible.

INTRODUCTION

Who really is this young, quiet Christian girl, Margaret Charlotte Gretschell, born on July 14, 1937 in Binghamton, New York, who ended up living in a quaint little place called Little Meadows, Pennsylvania, at eleven years old?

Born of a German father, Herman Gretschell, from Hanover, Germany, and an English mother, Charlotte Cosgrove, whose family came over from England on the Mayflower ship, it is indeed interesting and certainly calls for a story on how Margaret's life moved from this point into a life of ministry.

Margaret grew up with a younger sister and brother, Harriet and George. They were farmers and sold their milk each day after milking thirty cows. Her chores were daily and difficult, and her father relied on her to be his right hand. Imagine a thin, lovely, soft-brown-eyed girl with a movie-star smile, who had little physical power but large faith in Jesus and the courage of some biblical characters. As a teenager, she was involved in ministries out of Birchardville Baptist Church, which was the starting ground for shaping her for a life of ministry that God called her to. Her parents and Pastor Linebough and wife, Opal, encouraged her all the way.

She did well in high school, graduating as valedictorian, then went to nursing School in Johnson City, New York. At this same time, she was dating Garth Roberts and wearing his class ring; however, an engagement ring was on order. The word to describe physical and mental beauty was Margaret! And although people noticed these qualities, she was much more beautiful spiritually.

On April 28, 1956, she married Garth and through the years of her call to be a missionary, had five children of four girls and one boy. She lived on reserves for several years, teaching children, teens, and adults the Word of God. She overcame the challenges of opposition, children in crisis, raising her own children, jail ministry, cooking out-door in camps for several people for many years, being a pastor's wife and coping with her own personal struggles that her husband helped see her through. The workload was immense yet satisfying, and God received the glory.

Between the churches they pastored, serving children in crisis, summer and winter camps, and thirty-five years of jail ministry, many were saved and went on to a better life, some into ministry. However, at times, there was opposition from outsiders; but the armor of God proved itself, proving Him to be the Almighty God.

This spiritual mother to God's children, lived a full life, then left for her eternal rest in the Risen One and now lives on as He does, in heaven. Let's read on by rolling out the papered film of this faithful, delightful, and memorable woman, mother, spiritual mother, wife, and servant, whose life was lived for others in the presence of God.

"Rockin' in the Spirit of Love" is about Margaret Roberts, a Christian girl who became God's daughter at a young age, who became a woman, who became a wife and mother. Her story with some examples is about facing danger, as in accidents and surviving near death, adventure, as in a vacation with one of the largest street parties on the planet, opposition, as in plans on who to marry and when, health struggles, as in a career, or no career and increasing joy through it all.

The book reveals God's goodness and His victory in the life of this missionary who followed her calling. Every move of hers was motivated by her faith in her Savior Jesus Christ with a desire to be pleasing to Him by the end of each day. Her ministry included much prayer for the lives she was responsible for; God never misses a 911 call.

This book is meant to show the many blessings from God in ways that might help others to ponder what life as a missionary is about and to appreciate the fact that all have gifts and talents prepared by Him to carry out His will in the face of the world.

It's a "curl up on the couch" kind of book, so go ahead and laugh along with a cup of hot chocolate through the autumn and winter scenes and whatever you like for the spring and summer ones. Caution: you might near cry later, for God eventually takes home those who are His!

CHAPTER 1

On the Mountaintop

It's 1949–1950 in Little Meadows, Pennsylvania. A small-framed, eleven-twelve-year-old farm girl, born of Herman and Charlotte Gretschell, in Binghamton, New York, turned to her father to see which direction he was headed and whether or not it was time to come inside and get ready for church service. Sometimes there was something extra to be done outside.

They had just milked thirty cows, and Margaret was worried about smelling cow-ash whenever an outing was imminent. So she'd cover her head with a stink-proof shroud before doing the milking or cleaning the stable. She was quite pleased that she found a way to solve her problem and to be able to hold her head up high in church and sing like everyone else, and although Sunday services were held at home, they did get to church once a month thanks to a ride sent over for them. Eighteen miles was just too far to go with horses.

The shroud she wore was mostly for practicing with for school or if company was coming over. When the day would come for the family to own a car, her daydream was to let her hair ride on the wind from an open window. She had to walk two miles to her school and that helped to air out her hair in case any odor was lingering. Sometimes, if it was springtime, she would rub the early fragrant wildflowers between her hands and whirl them through her hair. But right now school was out, and summer was in!

The morning was particularly warm as the summer sun rose over the land filled with colored wildflowers that have been shivering all night. The white ones stood apart from the colored ones for some peculiar reason, and Margaret didn't like that. She thought they should all be growing up together, like the children she knew from different backgrounds.

While looking around for Dad and not seeing him, she shouted, "Hey, Dad, do white flowers get cold faster than the colored ones?" She figured there was something scientific about some colors holding more heat than others, something like how snow will melt faster under a tree.

Just as she realized he must be in the house, her attractive light-brown eyes spotted the first bumblebee of the day. He was marching wing by wing past her on his mission. "I wish I had a mission other than chores," she mumbled. "My chores are many and difficult."

Just then, she heard Mother calling for her to not be late for their service. "Coming, Mom," she shouted and accidentally brushed up against the pearly white flowers that suddenly had bees hanging all over them. They looked like they were hanging from ivory towers. One bee bounced to the earth, but she didn't notice because she was in a hurry to get to the house and look for her Bible.

With the fabulous sound of the screen door slamming behind her, Mother knew she was inside and motioned to her to eat her breakfast though it had been cold for some time. Every day everybody counted on that screen door for the same reason of either someone was coming or someone was going.

The sermon Father gave after breakfast was about sharing the gospel. Afterward, Margaret waited for Miss Snider to come over as was custom once every two weeks. She would gather the Gretschell children for Bible study. Miss. Snider was with child evangelism fellowship. Just then, Margaret suddenly realized that she was on a mission after all! She would learn much about Jesus, even more than she knew now. She would memorize the Bible like He did. Father started a fire under his daughter!

"Miss Snider is here now," called Mother.

Margaret came forward with her found Bible positioned perfectly in her hands, looking seriously at Mother and Miss Snider, who were very good friends. "I want to know everything Jesus said and did. He's the greatest teacher and I'd like to follow all His teachings," she said in earnest.

This was the day she hung a banner in her heart, "We will rejoice in your salvation, And in the name of our God we will set up our banners" (Psalm 20:5), and continued to learn Scripture alongside of her siblings, Harriet and George. Her parents watched her expand in knowledge, and they were pleased. Miss Snider encouraged the children each level of the way until one day it happened!

During one of the study lessons, Margaret willingly turned herself over to Jesus, putting her life and trust solely in Him. It was a mountaintop experience that would remain with her for life. Every day the mountainous joy not only grew larger but fuller with life in the Holy Spirit and keeping up with Him was a continual journey.

One quiet evening, while sitting with her Bible, she approached her parents and asked, "With my confession of faith in Jesus, how do I express that to my friends?"

"Just tell what decision you made and what resulted from it so far," answered Father.

"Well, I want to be baptized too," Margaret announced loudly, then became suddenly shy. It wasn't typical of her to be loud, but she knew she was saved and ready for the next step since she could identify with the meaning of baptism. She wanted to make a public declaration of surrendering her life to the Lord and her decision to be obedient to follow Him. And this all happened within a year.

When school started up again that fall in Meddle Town Centre, Margaret went back a changed girl. Oh, she looked like herself but felt different about her life. She had plenty of time to think about things on her two-mile walk to school, so she chose to reminisce a little, just to roll her memory over the things that took place that summer. It was a great year, and she knew more was to come. She recaptured the day of her baptism and some of the faces gleaming at her from the lawn they were standing on. She couldn't remember them all, but a handful of smiling faces jumped out at her. It was then that her memory rushed back with the water that flooded over her as Pastor Albert Whitehead baptized her in the creek behind Birchardville Baptist Church. It was a quaint little creek with a special purpose. (Two years after her baptism, Pastor Linebough became the new pastor.)

As she continued to the school, she thought of a well-structured sentence by Oswald Chambers that said something like this: "Never just stay on the mountaintop of wonderful experiences, but that you must go back down to the valley and deal with life there too." With that in mind, she believed God had a whole future laid out for her, and it began with her friends.

Upon arrival, Margaret was seen by the other girls who made a mad dash toward her and formed a circle around her. One girl stood on the tips of her fancy new shoes and, with both legs, tried to gracefully flare out her dress with a crooked ballerina twirl. The others rolled their eyes, then turned to Margaret and asked, "Margaret, what did you do for the summer break?"

"I worked with my Father on our farm and—"

But before she could finish, they clamored, "Oh we know, you were baptized behind Birchardville Baptist Church."

"Yes, and they were kind enough to pick up me and my family and take us home again," she said.

"Well, I was there you know. I saw your face disappear into the water. And I wondered if it would come out again, but it did." Margie, her closest friend, laughed.

"I wondered too." Margaret laughed. With the bell having rung, the girls darted for the old school door that the teacher was peering out of to see if any kids were still coming.

Once everyone took their places, books were opened, and work began. Margaret was a good student. She didn't like trouble of any kind and put forth much effort toward finishing her work on time.

Just then, a boy named Bernie, who sat across the one-room classroom from Margaret, flung his pencil toward her in hopes of getting her attention but got the attention of Mrs. Deweas instead. It hit the top of her glasses and toppled down her nose.

"Bernie, get in the corner," she demanded, with her finger pointing at the wall that stood kitty-corner to her desk. "That's three times this week you caused a commotion on behalf of your reckless choices."

Margaret knew he would just hatch a new plan to get her to notice him but wasn't interested in his boyish games. "I'm much too busy for him, and I don't like him anyway," she whispered to herself.

"Mrs. Deweas, can I get a drink of water?" asked Bernie.

"Go now before I change my mind, and make it fast," she said, in an authoritative voice.

Once outside, he charged for the window that was directly behind her back and dipped the ladle into the water basin. He lifted his beady eyes and pushed them against the windowpane, blinking them at the students, while holding up the ladle. Everyone looked with laughter, sending the teacher outside to look for him. He already had his head flipped back from the window and was sipping from the ladle. Later that day, she put a note in his parents' mailbox.

The bell rang out to end the school day, and some of the boys forged their way through the door to gather under the big white oak tree. That was the spot for planning. The girls gathered near the school's stairs. That was the spot for discussion. Two worlds collected into one classroom made for far too much interruption, so separation outside was welcomed by the girls.

After the walk home with Harriet and George, Margaret did her chores and wore her shroud just in case she couldn't wash her hair that evening. There was no school tomorrow, but someone could come for a visit on the weekend.

It was getting cooler out during the days now which made it harder for their hands to milk the cows, but Father relied on her to do her part. She was his hired hand when it came to the barn animals and taking the horses to buy feed. Mother relied on her to sweep the floors, do the dishes, and hang laundry when she couldn't. Harriet and George had their chores outside and inside too. Everyone pitched in on emptying the garden of its produce, then preparing the ground for next year. By the time the days were said and done, there was little time left for reading her Bible and homework. Margaret tried to read every morning and evening. She was growing in the Lord.

By this time, September, October, and November sailed past the people of Little Meadows, and Christmas was blowing in like a storm. Every year the Gretschell family would hurry to make gifts for one another and hide them until they were crafted and wrapped. Today was the forty-mile trip to the next town to shop for the stuff they had in mind from months before. Vestal, New York, was one of the two places they could get such things for Christmas. The other place was in Montrose. The trip to Vestal was cold and snowy, but it added to the splendor in the season of excitement!

Upon arrival, George swung over the horse sleigh and found himself half under the back end of it. He bumped Margaret on the way out, sending her into Harriet. Father pulled him out and warned him to calm down before entering the store, but he was a ten-year-old on a new frontier and too frivolous to be only a backwoods boy today.

A drove of children all belonging to a tired looking set of parents were racing each other to the store. They skidded past George and sneered at him. Margaret was trying to tell the difference between the boys and girls, but they all looked alike with their short hair. As everyone stood, looking at each other, Harriet took her opportunity to get into the store first, with Mom and Dad following behind.

The clerk was well prepared for the Christmas sales that always added up to be his most successful time of year. He had fancier candy than usual that kids would envision all year long—colored yarn, pretty material for making clothes, extra winter necessities, and toys, toys, toys!

To everyone's surprise, the children were calm enough to get through the shopping. No one wanted to be sent out to wait for their parents, therefore behaved in accordance with the expectations put on them. Margaret stood looking at the pretty white blouse and blue skirt in the window and imagined it on herself along with the matching shoes. It was a few sizes up from her size but could eventually fit her, she thought. Mother was studying the profile of her daughter's face and made a discovery. Margaret was heading toward her future at breakneck speed. George and Harriet had their own small amount of money to spend that they earned throughout the year and, after they secretly found what they were looking for, were sent out to the horse-bound sled. Mother and Father then grabbed the things they had already spotted and bought them. Together they smiled knowing the kids would be pleased on Christmas Day.

On the way home, they passed by the sneering kids who were bundled up in the hay on their sled. George was glad they didn't see him because they would just make strange faces that might stay with him the whole ride home. They struck him as unfriendly, and he wanted nothing to do with them.

The journey home seemed to be going quicker than it was in going to Vestal, Margaret thought. "Father, when we get home, do I have to do chores?" she asked.

"No, Mother will help me this time so that all of you can put your new things into hiding," he said softly.

"I'll need you to start supper though, Margaret," said Mother.

"I can do that for you, and I'll set the table. Maybe George can sit by Dad this time because he's been a fright to me lately. My arm is still hurting from when he flipped himself out of the sled, hitting it." Father chuckled until he remembered the full effect of the incident. Margaret looked over at George and Harriet who had hay tangled in their hair and wool mittens. She was not going to get any in her hair after the time she spent fixing it up for the shopping spree.

It was an exhausting but glorious day thought Margaret, as they turned the last corner for home. Her limbs felt icy cold and in need of the wood stove, but the outfit in the window was a warming picture that she framed in her mind.

Christmas was but two days away, and Margaret was ready for it. She had her gifts rolled in paper that she colored a design on and ribbons cut from gunny sacks for bows. She even made Mrs. Deweas a card with homemade bookmarks inside. The tree they cut down with Dad though was a difficult feat. The snow was deep, and Father had to visualize his steps before he made them. The kids followed in his oversized boot prints, and George measured his in one of them. This year he was happy with the result.

"Hey, Dad, there's a good tree to your left. It has a perfect top," he said, then made a cheerful jump into the snowy depths. When Father looked back to answer him, he was gone! The thick white stuff folded over him and buried his voice along with him. Harriet was pleased at his disappearance and forged her way over by Margaret. Together they giggled while they watched Father yank him out by one arm and one leg, then lift him into the air to shake him like a mat with dirt on it. On the way home, George thought of his boot prints getting closer in size to his father's; but to his fear, would his muscles?

Mother heard the screen door and stepped out of the way of the fallen Christmas tree. Father marched it through the kitchen to its resting place in the living room.

"What a bizarre little tree," she said.

"What do you mean?" replied Father.

"I mean that its fantastic. It reminds me of a tree I had growing up," she said with a smile. Everyone just realized that Mother was a kid at one time.

Christmas had come, and all gifts were under the tree that Mother so beautifully decorated. She built on it with strings of popcorn and cranberries. She dried out orange slices in the oven and hung them. Margaret always thought they looked like little suns and would swing one on its branch. Sometimes mother had extra slices for the kids to chew on.

She hung ornaments that were handmade from wood, but her most cherished decoration of all was the star for the top of the tree. It was her mother's favorite that her father handcrafted from aluminum surrounded with glossy fake pearls. When the light caught it just right, it became illuminated for that moment.

Father made a big dinner, and Mother put out the dinnerware kept just for special days. Most of the food was from their own farm animals, and a touch of summer was brought out in jarred vegetables from summer's garden. Father said grace, and later they sat around the tree to read Luke chapter 2.

The orange-red flames in the wood stove spread warmth around the family. The heat from the glowing embers ascended in waves, and sparks danced to the crackling sound of the dry logs. It was a godly atmosphere that bubbled over in the joy of the Lord.

When it was time for handing out gifts, Margaret wanted to give hers first. "Mother, this one is yours. I hope you like it. I think it'll suit you," she beamed.

"The wrapping is like a gift itself," said Mother as she carefully unwrapped it. "Oh, it's an apron and a broach. I especially love that you made one and bought the other!"

"Yes, I made the apron because I want you to feel a bit fancy like the pastry you make for us. Is it too fancy for you?"

With that question, Father laughed to himself about how Mother could use a bit of encouragement with the hours she spends in the kitchen.

"Yes, I think it'll complement me. Do I look ready for baking?" she asked after she tied it around herself, then put the broach on to show it off.

"You look right ready, Mother," said George while looking forward to eating whatever she bakes.

"Well look at this hat and socks," roared Father as he finished unwrapping his gift. "Just in time too because I lost my wool hat out hunting for the Christmas tree. And I need dry socks for tomorrow's chores." The girls looked at George as though it was all his fault for sinking himself into the snow, but he didn't notice.

George and Harriet were happy with their gifts of knitted socks and mittens from Margaret. Harriet promised to look after hers because she knew deep down that Margaret had a soft spot for her well-being. Margaret was a good sister, but being the oldest made life a little more difficult than theirs.

Mother and Father handed a gift each to George and Harriet. They ripped and tore at the paper till it was in shreds. One got a train set and the other a new dress with shoes. Harriet was in between being a little girl and a little lady. Mother figured a dress with shoes might help her decide where she's at. George was older but had the same problem of where he was at. He'd be okay once he stopped landing under sleighs and stirring up ideas with the boys at school.

George and Harriet presented their gifts to Margaret at the same time in the form of a note inside a card they made. When she read it, she almost couldn't believe it! It was filled with promises that they were both going to take over a chore each of hers. Harriet would sweep the house for her, and George would clean her share of the stable. But no one knew what to make of her expression, leaving each of them to think something different.

"This is really thoughtful," she said quietly.

"Well, we promise to keep our promises," they said softly.

The note said they'd do the chores for a month. With the talk of their opened gifts, everyone realized Margaret hadn't opened her gift from Father and Mother.

"Here's your gift that Mother and I bought you, darling. We felt it was something you hoped for, and Mother put her savings with mine to get it," he added.

Upon opening it, she saw her favorite color lay there before her. When she held it up, it unraveled, dropping to her lap. The other piece still in the wrapping was white. And Mother handed her something that completed the whole gift, a pair of shoes!

"I can't believe you both had enough money to purchase this outfit I saw in the store. How did you know I wanted it?" she asked.

"Mother noticed how many times you looked at it and told me. We know it's too big, but we bought it for your graduation. You can wear it for something special as soon as it fits you though. We just figured the store wouldn't have it by the time you graduate," he said, with a smile.

Margaret was thrilled with everything she got and shared her joy with her family until they were done singing and sharing their thoughts about another blessed Christmas. She crawled into bed too tired to remember to take off her slippers and tossed her blanket over her head. Her last thought was, *The earth is filled with His glory*.

CHAPTER 2

Two Birthdays and One Accident

Margaret continued to excel in everything she did for the next couple years. She was fourteen and in high school in grade nine at Rush, Pennsylvania. The chores were not much easier since her father was sick in bed. That was a scary time for the family, and during an attempt to milk the cows with Mother and harness the horses by herself, she nearly collapsed.

"I can't keep doing this without Dad," she cried to herself.

Just then, Andy Condon stepped inside the barn, looking down at this teeny, framed girl whom he thought must have the bravery like that of the biblical King David when he was a young boy.

"Where is your father at this troubled time of yours? Does he expect a girl of your stature to throw a harness overhead to reach the backs of these monsters when you can hardly lift one?"

"I can do this myself. And besides, my father is sick," she blurted out.

"What ails your father?" he asked.

"Pneumonia, and he would get out of bed to help me. But my mother won't let him, and I agreed."

The large Mr. Condon felt admiration for this teeny fourteen/ fifteen-year-old neighbor of his and took the harness from her and swung it up onto the horse like it was just a thought in action. From that time on, he helped her with her chores which made the days bearable until Father was better. And he did get better!

School was going well, but it was a twenty-eight-mile bus ride, making it dark out by the time she would get home. Mother seemed to be having a hard time in keeping up because of when Father was sick. She got behind on her stuff, such as sewing and laundry, in order to make trips for feed by way of horse and sleigh, as well as doing a few extra things that he would do. Margaret couldn't go for feed anymore because of the time she'd get home from school, yet somehow she and Margie still managed to meet in the barn to have their Bible study and talks about what to expect in high school.

Harriet and George had wood to bring in and stalls to clean out as usual, plus their schoolwork. Everyone pitched in with dishes after dinner so that mother could get to her waiting laundry. Sometimes Margaret helped with that too. The girls were able to sew well now and covered for Mother.

Margaret dreamed of going to church more often and to Young People's as she sat sewing. She needed to break out and run with others her age. She was going on fifteen with the independence of an adult. She had friends at school still, but that wasn't the same as her thoughts about being with like-minded believers who had the same desire for God. Little did she know until now that teaching Margie God's Word was just the beginning of her practice in ministry. It was from this time on that she figured her mission in life would be ministering to others under the direction of her Lord.

The next morning, Margaret decided she better wrap father's birthday gift. He needed a new axe handle that the family managed to pay for. His old one had been chiseled many times to re-fit the head and was no longer long enough to do it again. Mother was baking a cake, but every time she heard the screen door, she'd have to look like she was doing something different in case it was Father coming in.

During dinner, no one said a thing. George was slurping his soup, and Father finally put a stop to it. Mother narrowed her eyes at him, and Harriet rolled hers, then landed them on him again.

"Father, what day is it?" Margaret threw out there, hoping to jog his memory before something erupts at the dinner table.

"It's Saturday, isn't it? I'm pretty sure we go to church tomorrow. It's our week to go," he said.

"But have you seen what day on the calendar?" she said in pursuit.

"Yes, it's my birthday, and you all forgot it."

"No, we did not," cried Mother, as she had already slipped away from the table to get his cake.

"We have something for you," said George.

Harriet was waiting with her fork for a piece of cake that seemed to take too long to get to her. Mother lit one big candle, and they all sang out in different notes just like he remembered from the year before. Margaret handed him his gift that was kept in hiding under the table. He opened it and said, "Well now, it's not every day a man gets an axe handle from under a table. I think I need to find my axe head and attach it," he bellowed. But George had it in his hand, waiting for him to say just that very thing. Later George went out to stack the wood that Dad split.

As several months marched on, a new addition to the family came! Everyone was excited when it rolled into the driveway with Father grinning at them as they all stood motionless with their mouths open! Margaret was going on sixteen now and wanted to jump up and down and run around, but she felt it would make her look like a child. She believed in constraining herself if it meant acting age appropriate in front of others.

"Come see this machine," said Father, as he climbed out and slapped the car's door shut. Mother slipped inside on the passenger side and sank into the seat. The expression on her face was fresh again though she worked in the kitchen all day. Harriet and George fumbled with the door handles to get them open and bounced over one another to claim the same spot in the back seat.

At this point, Margaret dashed for the new 1946 family Ford and made a leap into the driver's seat, forgetting her stance on looking appropriate for her age, then looked back at the other two with a sense of satisfaction. She knew she was almost old enough, including responsible enough, to get her license. And that's exactly what happened some weeks after the new car came home.

"Well get in, everyone. Let's go for a ride," said Father.

They putted from neighbor to neighbor, their faces beaming out their windows. Margaret saw Bernie and looked away before he saw her. All she could think about was driving the car herself one day. When her sixteenth birthday would come, Mother and Father will have saved money for her to get her license. It was the perfect gift in their mind.

Meanwhile Margaret spent much time in the barn for privacy and special time. She read books and sometimes met in there with others. Her friends were still her friends, but Margie Swackhamer was her dearest friend! At nearly sixteen, they had more important things to talk about such as their future and driving to that future. The new car meant getting to Sunday school and to Young People's Group eighteen miles away, but for now, Father drove with her while she studied for her license.

With the warmer weather abound, they practiced together during the day on the farm. In the evenings, she spent her time day-dreaming about who God might bring into her life other than the friends He gave. God was number one and always would be, but she longed for what He had in mind for her.

The night before Margaret's birthday arrived that July, Mother stayed up to decorate. She didn't acquire much for the celebration because saving meant not spending; however, she and Father managed to find some lovely secondhand clothes that would fit her. She baked a cake, then iced it in blue and white. She hung a homemade sign that screamed happy birthday in large colorful letters.

That morning, when Margaret clasped the stair railing and skipped down to the last stair, she froze like a statue! The sign was staged on the wall directly in front of her. George popped out from nowhere, beginning to sing as everyone else came down from the top of the stairs. They handed her the gifts which turned out to be as lovely to her as was to Mother and Father. The day ended with a sixteen-year-old snuggled on the couch with her Bible and blanket.

Well, the days of studying paid off because Margaret passed the driver's test and would continue to practice with Father until he felt she was reasonably ready to venture out herself through the winding roads. Those roads would lead her into God's continued plan.

Margie came over that Friday prepared to learn more about the Bible with Margaret. Her parents would not allow her to go to church or to Young People's. She could only imagine it as Margaret told her how it was.

"Hey, are there any boys that I know who go to your church? I don't know because they never talk about it," asked Margie.

"Only two do, and they don't sing very well." Margaret laughed.

Margie's voice fell quiet because she was tired of asking and never seeing. "I'd be grateful if I could go even once to see for myself," she said as her brief smile dropped from her face, like every other time they'd discuss Margaret's godly privileges. "I'm probably going to marry a hermit like me and have baby hermits."

Just then, both girls roared with laughter, sending the farm animals in a flurry to find safety!

From the kitchen window, Mother saw chickens running for their lives and figured there was a fox nosing around. She sent Father to see what the commotion was. As he entered the barn, random feathers stuck to him, securing the idea of a fox in his barn. But all he saw were two sets of eyeballs blinking at him in wonder.

"What is it, Father? Did we laugh too loud?"

"Is that all that happened," he demanded.

"Why yes," exclaimed Margaret. "We were discussing how it is at church."

"Do you think you could ask my parents if I could go just once with you all to church, Mr. Gretschell?" interrupted Margie. As he began to relax, he agreed to ask if they would allow her to come with them on Sunday.

Upon entering the house, he saw his wife standing with a questionable look on her face. "Did you see anything?" she asked as she flashed her handheld knife in the direction of the front door.

"Yeah, just two girls whose laughter was powerful enough to frighten the chickens out of their feathers." He chuckled.

Just then, George came between them doing his clownish dance in search of attention. He was sent dancing to bed instead because the clock was about to strike nine. Father looked in on him to see if he really was in his room while Mother finished her day in the kitchen. Pies were made and dishes done!

"This has been a strange day to say the least," said Father as he reentered the kitchen.

"Indeed, it has been," replied Mother.

"I'm going to drive Margie home tonight and speak with her parents about the possibility of her coming to church with us," he said. At that moment, the screen door slammed shut the last time for Margaret that day as she entered the house. The others called it a day and went to their rooms. With lights out and the fire burning bright, it reminded Margaret of a burning she had of her own; what God has in store!

The next morning brought forth sunlight again just as God's divine Word said, paraphrased as, "The Lord commanded the morning and caused the dawn to know its place" (Job 37:12). And this would be a day to regard for the rest of Margaret's life.

"It's breakfast time," shouted Mother.

Margaret slid into her housecoat and slipped into her waiting slippers beside her bed. Her and Harriet's bedroom was awfully cool now that it was late September, and on the coldest nights to come, they would be sleeping on the floor downstairs next to the fire. The washroom used to be outside, and that was worse. It wasn't until she was sixteen that they had both running water and a washroom inside at the same time. Despite it all, she was nothing short of a lovely farm girl that had the grace of God to stand on. One look at her, and you'd think she had everything a teenage girl could want; well, she did. She had a rich relationship with Jesus!

On her way down to eat, she imagined it was her wedding day and tossed her arm onto the handrail of the stairs and lifted her chin as a sign of one who feels beautiful, like she heard of in the movies. With the other hand, she held up her housecoat as she would if it were a wedding gown. When she reached the bottom, she let her housecoat drop down over her slippers that posed as a pair of sparkling shoes that showed off her delicate feet. Everyone looked baffled as they watched her glide onto her chair and suspend her head like a statue.

"Darling, are you okay?" asked Father.

"I think so. I think today is special somehow, is all," she said, with elegance in her tone.

"Well, let's all bow and give thanks to the Lord," said Father, in his meaningful way.

Mother was beginning to recognize that her daughter was in a world within the world. She remembered behaving in the same way around the same age. She smiled to herself and, being the prayerful woman she was, thanked the Lord ahead of time for the perfect husband He would bring. However, once realizing how sad and empty home would be without her, she ended up tossing the conviction into the distance, for it was too realistic to consider. Sometimes her and Margaret had disagreements but not enough to want to give up the sound of her daughter's laughter or her ever-growing qualities.

George was scarfing down his breakfast while Harriet fixed her eyes on Margaret.

"May I be excused," Margaret groaned while trying to reclaim her imagined wedding gown. Her housecoat was caught on the table's leg making it difficult to stand up. George saw it and pulled the corner of it as hard as he could, sending the table in Harriet's direction. The glasses chimed like music, then collapsed because no one could catch them from the air in time.

"George, what in the world are you doing?" questioned Mother.

Harriet jumped out of the table's path, and the dishes flung forward as the table stopped just short of her, making her catch what was inevitably coming! Just at that moment, Father extended his arm as though he had another one attached to it and caught the "flying saucers." He even caught the "silver darts" that threatened to stick in Harriet.

Everyone fell quiet and stared at Father because of the impressive move he made. No one had ever seen him in that kind of action before. Mother couldn't even get angry over the situation because he caught nearly everything. And the five glasses that hit the tabletop ended up with only one of them broken.

"So this is our Saturday morning at breakfast!" Mother declared.

"It was George who did this, and at his age, it's just ridiculous. I could have been stabbed by a flying fork," barked Harriet.

"You're becoming a constant instigator, and it better stop," said Father in a stern voice.

"I'm sorry, Margaret. I pulled at you too hard. I'm sorry for everything, Mother," he said with ruefulness. This time, he had no grin on his face.

Maybe he will smarten up now, Margaret hoped, as she pondered the thought for a moment, then left the room to get dressed. She was going out that day to pick up four friends to go roller-skating.

"Father, I'm leaving with the car now. Can you tell Mother where I went in case she forgot? I think she's out back with the laundry," she said, then paused for an answer before skipping out the door with her roller skates. They were dangling from her hands by their straps. Suddenly, she froze. It had snowed through the night, but no one said a thing about it earlier!

During the skate, Bernie popped up by Margaret to say hi. By this time, he was a bit less annoying by about eight ounces, but he still had another cup of trouble in those beady eyes of his. She could still see them pushed up against the window in grade school. *I'll bet Mrs. Deweas still sees his pencil on the end of her nose*, she thought, giggling out loud.

Bernie looked puzzled. He thought she was laughing at him because he wasn't so great on skates. He never really knew her to laugh at anyone, he thought to himself. She then skated off to catch up with her friends for the last lap around the rink for the night.

On the way home, they sang Christmas songs though it was almost three months away. Right now, it felt like Christmas because of the freedom provided by the car to get around in. Margaret stopped singing when she saw the hairpin corner coming closer. She never had too much trouble with it so far, but ice buildup was inevitable which she knew from her driving lessons.

All singing halted from the others as though the notes dropped off their tongues and hung in midair only to return once the corner was behind them, but they never finished rounding the corner.

Margaret shrieked, followed by a stream of high-pitched shrills from the others. The corner sucked them in and enveloped the air with snow.

Four tires were facing heaven, spinning in the cold air in resistance to the power train of the upside-down car. The sound was ungodly between that and the shrills. They weren't sure which way was up or down. The roll flattened their hair, and it wasn't until they saw the roof of the car reaching for the back of their heads that they realized it landed upside down.

By the time Father was notified, they were standing on the road, waiting to be rescued. He drove up with his friend, and three other men came to help. They pushed that car back over onto its tires like it was made from cardboard.

"Are you all okay?" asked Father. They looked fine, but he asked anyway, knowing that they must be shook up.

"We are, but the car..." Margaret said, trying to muster up enough of a voice to finish her sentence.

"Don't worry, it'll be all right once the oil drains back down. After that, I'll start it, and it should run clean again. In the meantime, I must fix the roof," he said. He climbed in his overturned car and laid on his back, positioned his feet, and held his breath. With multiple tries, he reshaped its sagging roof. Margaret didn't know what she'd do without him. She and Father were very close. The corner that lies in wait for oncoming cars made them even closer. And that was how she decided to look at the incident.

The others were taken home to their waiting parents. Mother was overwhelmed but glad no one was hurt. She approached Margaret with her arms out to give her a hug and to look her over. "Are you hurt anywhere?" she asked.

"No, but I'm tired. I think I'll go to my room," she replied. She sat on her bed and flopped over, missing her pillow altogether.

CHAPTER 3

The New Face

With the rolling in of October, it was time to start crafting for Christmas. Ideas were flying through Margaret's mind on what to make this year. She was given enough bundles of yarn by a neighbor whose hands were too aged to knit with anymore. She could make a throw blanket for the couch for Mother. She'd even have enough to knit her new slippers.

Father was easy because he always seemed to lose his knitted hat from the Christmas before while tree hunting, but come every spring, no one could find it! She'd make him another one in a different color.

She had enough money for fancy candy for George and Harriet and possibly a good book to read for each of them. The greatest part she loved was that God gave the ultimate gift. She believed all other gifts were supposed to stem from the act of giving more than from receiving.

That Friday, Father drove her to Young People's. "I'll be back to pick you up," he said.

"Okay, I'll be inside in case you're a bit late. Pastor Dale waits with anyone who's still here," she said as she hurried to slam the car door.

The pastor was sitting with his preparations in hand as the teens came in. The lesson tonight was about their unchanging God. Margaret managed to ask all her questions on the topic afterward because Father was twenty minutes late. It was then that he decided to let her drive herself from now on.

The following Friday, she showed up in the family Ford looking like a movie star, but not acting as one. Her natural look was lovely. You could spot her soft brown eyes sparkling from across a room. Her teeth made her face look radiant, and her lips carried a built-in smile that held the kind of shape you might see in a portrait done by a famous painter. Some called it a smile to remember, but it was purely by God's hand that He was the artist who painted her to be this way; further, He tucked into her a heart of good treasure, "A good man out of the good treasure of his heart brings forth good" (Luke 6:45).

As she parked, others were being dropped off by their parents. She could see arms extended with waving hands at the ends of them. She raised hers to wave back as she swung herself out of the driver's seat, recalling the years she waited to drive to these Friday nights.

Everyone met in a pile at the door to go in together, Margaret being first to enter. Pastor Dale greeted them with one long smile as usual upon their entry and pointed to the papers on a table for everyone to take on their way by. The lesson tonight was about how to share God's Word with unbelievers.

It wasn't long after Margaret had been helping Pastor Dale Linebough's wife, Opal, with the junior class of children aged eight to thirteen that she knew it was her ministry from the Lord. That was on Tuesdays, plus still attending her own night on Fridays. Her heart was in anything to do with teaching and helping in various ways. Pastor Dale and Opal were a huge part of Margaret's first experience in ministry. They were responsible for encouraging her to cultivate her relationship with Jesus. Her parents backed her all the way because they loved the Lord as well.

That Sunday morning, Margaret's blankets became airborne as she stretched out her restless legs from a long cold night. They crashlanded at the end of Harriet's bed, waking her with an oblivious look on her face.

"What's happening?" groaned Harriet.

"Nothing. I just hate when my blankets crawl around my legs, cutting off their freedom from the rest of me." Margaret laughed. It was totally a laughable scene, but Harriet wasn't impressed.

"Well, you better keep your flying blankets to yourself," she growled.

Margaret lifted her slender body out of bed to swirl her housecoat over her nightgown. It floated to her Cinderella feet which complemented her worn slippers as she gracefully stepped into them. The wood stove was bellowing with heat and warmed her before she began to cook breakfast for everyone.

The cows were already being milked for reason of both Mother and Father chore together on some Sundays while Margaret cooked. Today she made pancakes and set the table with Mother's homemade syrup and butter. They sat on the warming plate until the table had everyone gathered round it.

Being October, the drive to church was cool and colorful. Some leaves were still stuck on branches with a thick layer of sparkling frost and hints of wet snow. The sun was doing its best to melt what it could before the freeze came again over night. Birds were perched on the skinniest of warm twigs, singing to each other. It made autumn look forced to greet winter and to give it place over the next several weeks. The wind picked up the loose leaves and took them as far as the valleys. The river carried its share into the unknown, and the rains pelted the rest into the ground.

The roll over from that September through October had its unique way of changing the leaves from colors of green to faded green, then yellow. Some were bright red and orange. They all eventually turned brown as the season went on. Some remained clung to the bush, but many lay in silence in the darkness under blankets of snow. Margaret understood this turnover of seasons because of her interest in chemistry, biology, and science. High school was the platform for the knowledge she needed to begin her career afterward.

She was very familiar with the sun's effect on nature as well when it came to chlorophyll and regrowth. She pictured the season of spring pushing up stems of new flowers again and buds exploding into leaves that were already on certain trees as a second set. They replace the fallen ones that already lived out their life. In the winter, they are sleeping buds tightly rolled up on the branches awaiting spring.

She thought about how ants crawl on certain large flowers and lick the nectar off before they open to face the world of other pollinators. There were many lovely things to think about on the way to church.

"We're here. Who's ready to si—" Father almost asked. He recalled the different notes that made up his birthday song and changed his mind on what he was about to ask. "George, open mother's door for her. Harriet, take and fold the car blanket you used," he ordered.

Margaret broke out of her door to help Mother walk because she was nursing a wound on her leg from falling in the barn. It was red and a bit swollen. The pastor was waiting to open the door for them as soon as they reached the top step.

"Good morning, Mrs. Gretschell. I see you have your leg bandaged. I hope it's not too painful," he said in a comforting voice.

"It's not so bad. I just didn't want anything to get into the wound, so Margaret wrapped it up for me."

"Yes, and she did a good job, just like a nurse would," said Father.

"Well, we could use more nurses here," said the pastor.

George walked past everyone to claim a row seat for the family, then parked himself on the pew. It was in front of a new face in church! He was about Margaret's age and was sitting ten pews behind.

After songs were sung, the pastor began to pray. One of the things he asked for was physical healing for those who needed it. Mother felt father's elbow touch hers. They were warmed at the thought of how caring their pastor was.

Contrary to Father's belief, his family harmonized well on the last song of the morning. No haunting looks from anyone today. It was mostly George anyway who missed notes or sang them out of key. Either he sang too high or too low. It was nice when he didn't sing at all, thought Harriet. However, Father did want him to participate, just not too loudly. Each Sunday was a surprise in the making.

It took some of that month for the new face in church and Margaret to talk. His name was Garth Roberts, and when they finally got past the shy hellos, they were able to communicate sentences. He lived in Montrose and was going to high school there. Birchardville Baptist Church lied in between them. Anyone could see that she had a sunny face when he was around, and he surrounded himself with every minute of her attention that was possible. Mother's eyes were never far away; they kept a mental note after every Sunday. She was seeing it again, that look of in a world of her own, in the world.

Father was strict but knew the day would come for his daughter to move into a life of her own and do the same thing he did at the age of independence. He was happy at the idea if she married the man God chose. Mother preferred to choose the man though she tried to give God the reins.

The beginning of December arrived full blown with snow. Margaret and Garth had been dating since their decision on October thirty first. He was telling Margaret about his school bus's chained tires after church. It was 1954, and that was basically a bus rule for safety. She marveled at his storytelling because she loved reading and thought he was good at telling it the way it is.

Mother's eyes were floating around the room, picking up everything in their path and discarding it until they found Margaret. It was because of a rumor she heard about the young man's family that might be of importance if her daughter was going to stay friends with him. Father heard too but knew judging someone with someone else's judgment was a way of putting a middleman in place of his own moral judgment; it's wrong. He and mother had things to discuss later that day.

George and Harriet took little note of their sister's friends. They had their own new acquaintances to get to know. George was fourteen now and was still in and out of bits of trouble at home and at school. Father managed him well though. He kept him busy with chores and had longer conversations with him.

Harriet being twelve would soon give mother a busier set of eyes to keep up on the whereabouts of both daughters. But Margaret was a proper girl who was devoted to Jesus for her needs. Mother knew this but had a hard time letting her eyes rest.

Christmas was finally here, and the family had their traditional celebration, with a guest! Margaret swung the dried oranges on the tree that to her, still looked like little suns. She wondered if Garth would like the card she got him. She knew he'd keep it close to his heart because he always kept even the smallest moment that they shared close.

"Who wants to start unwrapping their gifts?" chimed Father.

"Let's give our guest the first gift this evening," said Mother. Mother wanted to be the one to hand him their gift. Everyone sat entirely without sound. George and Harriet were tight-lipped because they didn't even know what he was getting. Garth slowly unwrapped it as though he was trying to pull the wrapping without hurting it. It isn't easy being in a household that is leery about you.

"This is just what I needed. I needed a Bible! And I couldn't have found a nicer one than this," he declared. Mother perked up and smiled at him.

It turned out that Margaret and Garth had hope after all of Mother's affections ever becoming a reality. The other gifts were opened amid family as the blazing fire eventually left behind glowing embers. Then another log was added before they crumbled into ashes.

The turkey was devoured mostly by Dad and George. Harriet had little daydreams of her own about the future while Mother sat admiring her starry treetop that her Father made when she was a girl. Margaret and Garth sat together almost too happy to speak. They spent some time just absorbing the evening, holding their Christmas card from each other. Everyone told what they liked about the church play that the three of them and Garth took part in. It was his first Christmas as a Christian, therefore his first Christmas play. Margaret was a major leader in the youth group presentation. All involved did a wonderful work on the story of Christmas. Following that was a bag of candy and an orange to bring home. Margaret was deeply involved in church. She taught children in Sunday school and went faithfully to Young People's. This is where her life excelled, propelling her into the life chapter of godly love!

CHAPTER 4

Becoming a Woman

The Gretschells didn't have a phone yet. Messages had to be brought home from school or church unless it was important enough to use the car. Margie was not allowed to come to church yet and still met in the barn with Margaret to discuss church events. Young People's was on her agenda, but it wasn't happening yet either.

Margaret was still bringing Harriet to the junior youth group. George was now old enough for the senior group at Young People's. Being fourteen, he was thrilled to be with the older boys.

Margaret and Garth were still dating on the premise that they would read the Bible and pray together and apart. She read him her lifelong memory verses of Proverbs 3:1–6 during a hayride that was put on by the young people of their church. It would be a ride to remember for many reasons as the large sturdy team of Lester Hay's horses smashed through the snow and ice with their powerful hooves. They carted that sleigh up and down hills like they were little snow drifts or moguls. Lester was the deacon of their church who loved to cart people around.

Margaret proved to be consistent and loyal in her faith, but Mother was still steering her eyes in the wrong direction. Garth kept his eyes on Margaret too. He still thought she was too lovely to have though her heart was saying different. It would have done mother better had she not used her ears or her eyes at all. Father always said, "What we hear isn't always what we think we're seeing." Margaret's parents loved her and were so committed to providing for her that they wondered who best could replace them.

In the coming days, she and Garth found it harder to stay apart until the next Friday, then Sunday, and would sometimes meet at her place, but it wasn't that often because her parents weren't too keen on the idea. Sometimes they'd talk in the barn to get away from Harriet and George and fretful mother. It now being a Saturday meant two days in a row to see each other.

"Well, I better start for home," said a hesitant Garth.

He and Margaret had a brief hug for him to take on the long ride home. He replayed it in his mind a hundred times. Times like that could linger for several years when its true love and never fade away.

Margaret played out her memory of it in slow motion on the staircase. Coming down, it always seemed to be the runway for her imagination. It was the runway of the future. No one used it the way she did. She's a serious and hardworking girl with an interesting way of unraveling her character. She knows how to have fun even if sometimes it's serious fun; after all, dreaming about marriage is serious!

The Christmas holidays are over with high school back in. Getting closer to seventeen meant getting nearer to grade twelve. The coming summer would be her last summer of high school holidays. Her plan afterward was to go to nursing school. She could see herself as a part of the medical structure for following the protocol of a diagnosis and treatment. The collaboration of doctors and nurses was appealing to her in the personal healing of patients. She loved practicing on her family, such as the time Mother fell in the barn.

One morning, during her bus ride to school, she saw George sticking his nose in Sam's hair. Sam is a girl with arms strong as clubs. Messing with her could put his nose out of joint thought Margaret, so she tried to get his attention but was too late! Sam grabbed his head, pulling it forward into the back of her seat, and held it there until the bus driver looked up in his mirror. He was lucky it was only a moment. When she let go, Margaret saw the imprint of his face. She was sure skin cells were mingled in it. No blood though!

Margaret's thoughts shifted to Garth and wished he was on her bus and in her school to work with and have lunch with. Bernie sometimes tried to sit by her during lunch, but the other girls kicked at him under the desk the second he sat down. After that incident, however, he gave up and focused on a girl with brilliant dark eyes like his. They looked cute together thought Margaret as she'd watch them stroll off. She was glad he may have found a match for him. Of course, some laughed at the idea of beedi babies in their future, but Margaret didn't respond.

The ride home went better for George. He kept his nose in his seat. Once they were home, they did chores as quick as possible because it was Friday. Garth had been attending her group which gave her the energy she needed to clean the stable before she could go. They had to add George to the recipe as of a while ago since he was old enough now for Fridays at Young People's. She and Garth took Harriet and his younger siblings to their youth group on Tuesdays which gave another few hours for them to be together.

Both of their hearts stayed warm over the winter with memories after each visit. Mother and Father saw this and became more acquainted with their relationship that took place in church, at Young People's, and the outdoors, meaning the barn of less interruptions by kids. They had to discuss their lives! This being 1954, he had pledged his faith in Christ and was saved by Christ, which gave much to talk about. It happened that February fourteenth when his life was changed forever. They studied the Bible many times in that old, cold barn that served as a place of ministry. Margaret shared what she had learned throughout her years with Miss Snider until they caught up to where they were presently at. And that was how the rest of winter went.

When the spring sun began peeking over the hills and into the valleys, their school year was running out of days. Soon the rotted leaves from under the snow were exposed, then gave way to new plants springing through their composted remains.

Margaret still had little kids trailing behind her in the children's Sunday school and the hope of a future with Garth. Then there was his mother who loved her and did all she could to help her and Garth as far as support went. Few looked at the young couple as a hope in progress. God looked at them as a light to others. Mrs. Roberts mothered Margaret every way possible like she was her own daughter. Garth appreciated every moment those two spent together talking about the woman Margaret was becoming.

With the end of grade eleven, Margaret achieved high marks in all her subjects. She could foresee herself doing the same in her senior year to come. Life wasn't just drifting anymore; it was rocketing from one season to the next.

That summer brought in bunches of butterflies floating from one wildflower to another. Birds of all shapes and sizes were practicing their runway skills for when their real attempt to fly was inevitable. It was either fly or die. God spilled grass over the bare ground and watered it with the wells in clouds, and Margaret could see that He gave it all. It reminded her of God giving His only begotten Son which she knew meant one of a kind, or only one, and He spared no expense for us; it cost Him His life! That's the one debt we don't have to pay, she thought with admiration.

It was during one summer evening when Margaret's parents came to talk with her about her plans at the end of high school. It was a little early seeing as she had her senior year to do yet. "Margaret, Mother and I are prepared to help you after your last year of school. You are doing well enough by far for your enrollment in nursing school later. We need to know what all it requires for you to go," he said with affection. They were also thinking she should put her focus on her career before her relationship with Garth.

"I'm not sure yet. I need to speak again with the school advisor. He's the counselor who will be talking to everyone this coming year about our plans," she said, with reassurance that her plan for nursing was still her number one choice.

"We would like to know when that takes place," said Mother.

"All right, I'll let you both know," she replied.

"Now what about Garth? You will have to go to the Wilson Memorial Hospital in Johnson City, New York, and stay there in residence," Father suddenly said with less affection now.

Mother jumped in to add, "Well, he'll have to move on because you'll be so busy, and nothing can be an interruption for you."

"Is that what you think he is, nothing but an interruption? It wasn't that way with you and Father. Well, I love the interruption. It's the best kind in life!" she said in a standoff position. Her heart was pounding with the realization of what her parents put on her which was that her love for someone other than her family was apparent, and they saw that.

It was pretty much the last time they tried to speak of her and Garth's relationship as temporary. To influence her would be to gripe with the wind. Margaret was a humble but feisty young lady when it came to right and wrong, and there was no wrong in feeling the beginnings of love for someone whom she felt had special qualities. Just as important was the fact that he cared deeply for her and God. She could build a marriage on that! Now that was a plan. She was not forsaking her career, Garth, her ministry in church, or God, not even her parents, by her choices.

With summer abound in newness, Margaret continued to put all of herself into her ministry at church. She taught the children to see how Jesus's life went step by step with each one leading to multiple parables, several miracles, and numerous ways in which He shows His love. She based it all on the fact that the ultimate way was His death. His birth, death, and resurrection gave much hope to their little hearts. It's always been a heroic thing to die for someone such as a passerby trying to save someone and not succeed, but when it comes to Jesus, it's hard for others to believe why He chose day after day to put Himself in danger of the cross; to die for sinners wasn't out of instinct. He acted out of pure love. She conveyed His message to them with clarity.

Driving home from picking up feed that Thursday, Margaret turned the car around and spun off in a quick decision to go to Mr. and Mrs. Roberts' place instead. Not only was his mother supportive, but his father fully accepted her too. She felt comfortable around them and wanted to see Garth to tell him something. Upon arrival, she waved in the window as she rolled into their driveway.

"Hello, Margaret. Are you here for a visit?" asked Mrs. Roberts.

"Yes," she said as she dropped her hand to open the car door. "I came to ask if we could all have dinner together some time. I could bring a salad after church this Sunday."

"That would be…" Mrs. Roberts began to say.

Just then, Garth came out of the house with his shoes in a shamble. He was hurrying to meet with her. He hadn't seen her since Tuesday, and to him, that was like a month.

"Hey, is everything okay?" asked Garth.

"Yes. I wanted to see how you're doing and to ask you all about having dinner here on Sunday. I'm free after church," she announced. She wasn't sure about being free to use the car for her purpose with her parents possibly stubborn at the idea.

"Well, I like that concept," said Mr. Roberts with crossed arms and a grin on his face.

"And I as well," agreed Mrs. Roberts.

"Okay, I'll see you then," said Margaret as she walked closer to Garth. They stood in the summer sun that shot glimmering rays through the trees onto the ground. Particles in the air were swirling between them. A puddle from an earlier rain sat still, then rippled with a breeze, making it hard to see the reflection of the passing clouds. When the breeze died down, silence ruled for but a moment. Not one minute is the same as the last. And to recapture the last is to reimagine it only, thought Margaret as she examined the picturesque view they were standing in.

"I suppose I better be leaving now. I came here unexpectedly," she said without regret.

"I'm glad you came. It surely was unexpectedly of you," he said, smiling at her sunlit face.

"My parents aren't overjoyed about us. That's another reason I came to see you. Father used to be more accepting, but I think he's just worried about me getting a career. Mother is disturbing herself over my choices because she doesn't like the things she's been hearing," Margaret calmly said.

"Well, I can't help how she feels about my family, but I've been showing her how I will always treat you, if that's been helping at all," he said. They both stood in the sun's rays absorbing them as they continued to streak through the trees with particles teeming in unpredictable motion.

"Well, I better be leaving," she said a second time.

"We can have a prayer first. The Lord can do wonderful things when it comes to parents," he suggested as they stood melting in the rays in one another's arms. They prayed, and she then took a princess step in the direction of the car. Though there was no royalty in her bloodline, she did serve her Lord with a royal heart. "Know the God of your father, and serve Him with a royal heart and with a willing mind; for the Lord searches all hearts and understands all the intent of the thoughts" (1 Chronicles 28:9).

On the way home, she made it clear to the hairpin corner that she wasn't going to put up with its threat. She spoke to it like it was lying in wait for her as usual, "You are just one of the things in life that tries to pull me in the wrong direction. I've become sharper than you. If only my parents would bend like you though, I'd be grateful, but only Jesus could make that happen."

Father was outside when she arrived, and to her surprise, he wasn't upset at how long she's been gone. Chores were waiting for her more than her parents were!

"Hello, darling, we need to do the milking. I'll clean the stalls with George afterward because Mother needs help with laundry," he said.

"All right. I got the feed in the car for you to lift out. It was nice to be able to use the car this time instead of the horses. I like when we need less feed because of summer," she said with a sparkle in her eyes. Father knew she was visiting Garth; her eyes said so.

"Yes, this car is an answer to many things," he replied.

Mother was equally friendly to her but also noticed her sparkling eyes. "Margaret, I'll be needing help once you're finished outside," she said, as she directed her eyes to the lovely daughter she had.

"Not a problem, I'll be as quick as I can," she said, then hopped to it.

When Sunday came, everyone was settled at the table, waiting for their parents to join them in breakfast. It was Margaret's turn to cook. The pancakes never looked so good to George who was sticking his nose once again where it didn't belong. Harriet was annoyed with him and flicked her finger in his face. Margaret suddenly realized that they still look and act the same as ever. She could be leaving home in a year and a bit, and they'd still be sneering at each other. Just then, the screen door played its one note tune, one big bang! Breakfast was consumed with George depositing the most into his bowling-alley belly.

Garth and Margaret sat together in church, which was becoming a common picture, but a godly one. The pastor spoke about entering marriage God's way. It was a perfect message to parents about their children. Margaret trusted it came from Jesus! Garth wished his parents were there to hear it because they would have agreed.

Going home afterward was a complete disaster for Mother. She came to realize that her desires for her children were just that, her desires, not God's. She felt she was wrestling with God instead of before God. Her heart was not put before Him to change. God's great writer, Oswald Chambers, said, "You must learn to wrestle against the things that hinder your communication with God, and wrestle in prayer for other people; but to wrestle with God in prayer is unscriptural. If you ever do wrestle with God, you will be crippled for the rest of your life." He goes on to say, "Wrestling before God makes an impact in His kingdom. And if you grab hold of God and wrestle with Him, as Jacob did, simply because He is working in a way that doesn't meet with your approval, you force Him to put you out of joint (Genesis 32:24–25)."

After all, she did pray earlier in Margaret's life for the husband God would bring!

CHAPTER 5

A Double Graduation

Little by little, autumn forged its way in to begin fashioning the leaves with color. Margaret thought it as though God beautifies them not only in their life, but in their last days. He does the same thing with Christians, except a saint's death is more precious in His sight. Precious in the sight of the Lord is the death of His saints (Psalms 116:15).

Many of the leaves skipped along the ground in the wind, but some raced with bigger winds into the rivers and lakes. Pine cones dropped to the ground for burial so that winter could do its job in covering everything until the power of summer could resurrect new life from them.

Margaret was enthused with school being in and moving along like she expected. Grade twelve is largely critical. "'Taking time to make time might be possible, but with all the things going on with school and ministry, that phrase may not be sustainable," she said aloud to herself.

When she arrived in class, her teacher sat staring at papers. "Margaret," called Mrs. Milford.

"Yes, I'm here today," she replied, looking up from her books.

"I have your chemistry test results, and I believe you'll be quite happy with it," she beamed as she strolled over to her desk with the test.

"Thank you, that is good news. My parents will want to see it," she said quietly as she reached for the paper from her hand. Margaret wasn't one to brag about herself and was hoping no one was paying attention to her at that moment. There was one girl named Claire who would marvel at her, then make an advertisement with her face as if to say, "Big deal." But Margaret was waiting for the right time to share her faith when her and Claire could be alone.

The bus ride home sent Margaret to sleep against the window. Her books slid one way, then the other. She slept until a bump hoisted them from the seat and left them teetering at the edge when they landed. She stretched forward to try to reclaim them in time from falling to the wet floor, but Claire caught them first. She was watching Margaret sleep and seemed to be developing a change of heart toward her.

"I saw your books sliding around and was going to wake you, but it didn't seem important enough till they were teetering," she declared.

"I'm glad you caught them for me. This floor is smeared with a bit of everything," she said with relief.

"Well contrary to what you may think, I don't dislike you enough to allow your work to mingle in the mire," she remarked.

"Thanks, Claire. Only a decent person would do that for another."

"So what's up with that churchy talk you have about you?" she blurted out.

"You mean speaking with boldness yet kindness?" said Margaret, with a smile.

"Yeah, something like that. You're never confused or rude."

"I don't have to be. I know the way I need to be as long as it pleases God."

"Why would you wanna please someone you can't see or talk to?"

"But I do see God and talk to Him. I see Him all through the Bible, and I pray."

"Have you had any answers?"

"All the time," said Margaret.

"If you can tell me why someone would die for me, I'll consider thinking about Him more," she plainly said.

Margaret ministered to Claire every bus ride home starting with the analogy to Christ of why she would save her books from the mire.

The snows came and went. Chains came off the school buses, and spring promised freedom from the cold blizzardy days. The warm rains stirred up the ground to bring out the frost, and soon farmers could replace weak fence posts and turn the ground over for new gardens. But Margaret's favorite of all, it's the time for everything to come to life! It reminded her of a poem she memorized from a friend who shared it with her. It begins by lifting your heart, then ends by dropping it, but picks out the seasons of spring and fall. She recalled it on one of her bus rides home.

I Remember

I remember a time so clear, you and I by the beavers' pond,
We watched a family of several deer and how they took care of the youngest fawn.
The wind was spreading all new seeds…you know the job it has come fall, then spring.
Soon it was hard to see over the weeds and the greatest of songbirds came to sing.
Pretty lilacs avoided shade for light, their strength in design is in their base.
They shift in the day breeze and sit still in night, then burst at dawn into petals of lace.
The moose settled under nearby trees, everywhere, stood pearly wildflowers.
They were helping countless tired bees who looked like they were hanging from ivory towers.
I remember a time so great, when it was just you and I,
We sat by the fire till it grew late, watching the stars light up the sky, but… I never dreamed this life would die.
Today the beavers have left the pond, and the dear are of few.

They let go of the youngest fawn, now it lays in the cold morning dew.

The wind grew so fierce and cold, the wildflowers are sure to die.

The wilted weeds are put on hold, and the birds can hardly fly.

The scent of lilacs has long faded, and the moose are all on the run.

You and I are so outdated…love…is no more fun.

S. S.

The bus jeered to a stop, and Margaret lifted her books, hugging them as she looked down before taking the first step. The poem left her in limbo, wondering how love can be as lively as spring, then turn cold like fall. "God would see to it that my life would be different," she concluded in her private thoughts.

She and Garth were moving fast forward with their graduations at hand. Talk of marriage was on the table, God's table! Mother and Father were scrambling to finalize her payment for first year of nursing come fall. Margaret had some money of her own saved for something special. George and Harriet came at a price too. They needed new shoes and more food to fill the alley in George's belly. Father told him he'd have to help more in the garden from now on. Harriet was in between the age of chasing butterflies and boys. By now, Mother's eyes began taking rest stops whenever Garth was present. That helped Margaret to feel respected, and not the least bit resentful anymore.

Less than two months of school left, and Margaret surprised her parents with her marks that were higher than hoped for. She was still doing everything right in her life, and God was rewarding her in ways seen and unseen. Claire decided to believe Jesus to be real, but George and Harriet weren't there just yet. Margie was finally able to attend church, but only occasionally. She was dating with plans to marry as well. She would soon be able to attend church by her own decision.

It's June 1955, and graduation was finally happening for both Margaret and Garth. Of course, they attended different high schools;

however, their ceremonies were on different nights, so they were able to go to one another's grad.

Margaret sat in her room looking at her blue skirt with the white blouse and shoes she received a few Christmases ago. Her parents were waiting downstairs to see her in the outfit they bought her. She never did wear it anywhere else before grad night like her parents suggested.

Garth met her once she arrived for the ceremony. He had a card for her. Margie was waiting for her too and hurried toward her with her card.

"I cannot believe you are valedictorian, Margaret," sang Margie.

"You said I would be, remember?" Margaret laughed.

"Yeah, but it really happened. You are valedictorian," she repeated, still singing the words.

"I believe it and always knew it," boasted Garth.

Excited voices filled the building. Young men and women stood all over. It was an array of colors. A display of smiles was everywhere, including those of the gratified parents. Everyone put on their grad gowns and hats as it was about to begin!

With each name called, cheers bellowed from the audience. The entire evening was littered with joyful chaos. But it never got out of hand.

So much happened that year, and things were not about to slow down. Garth was baptized that March before their grads, which made her parents a lot happier.

After her grad, Mrs. Roberts continued to be Margaret's mentor into womanhood. Their relationship is as adorable as Margaret herself. They spend Sunday afternoons together as often as they can to discuss the future and what marriage really means. Margaret is good at looking and thinking forward. Scripture has built her mind from the bottom up. That's the way God works; He lifts you up toward Himself until you're on track with Him, then guides you through your salvation. The end of life is simply the final step to Him, she believed. Thanks to Miss Snider, her parents, Pastor Dale, and his wife, Opal, her biblical knowledge at her age is amazing.

Summer was in the air, and Margaret with her graduation behind her had been accepted by the school of nursing in Johnson City, New York. She had just weeks to finish planning and get there in residency. Going to Mrs. Roberts's house that Sunday was the first place she thought of going to share her news. "The Wilson Memorial Hospital sounds so real to me now," Margaret said as Mrs. Roberts took measurements of her kitchen window. It was time for a new curtain. Margaret was helping her and did the math in her head.

"Well, I know you'll do well just like when you were in high school. I'm not concerned about that part of it," she asserted.

"But I'm concerned about mine and Garth's decision to get married. I'm not sure how it'll all fit in yet with my career. My parents want me to do things differently, but I'm relying on God to connect it all," she said, with a voice that suddenly dropped off, then came back with a vengeance.

"That's it, I'll just do what comes next, and He'll steer me as I go. I don't know why I'm getting worried anyway when He has it under control."

"Your God will do just that," said Mrs. Roberts, agreeing with her, then realizing for the first time that all along, He was using

Margaret to her advantage because every time she was around, so was He.

Mrs. Roberts was saved as a teenager and had a spot in the choir, but life twisted a different way after getting married. She hadn't been to church since the age of twenty-one, hence Margaret's life bringing God alive in hers again.

"Enough of this curtain! Let's have a piece of pie with tea. I would like to make your wedding cake. I think you should have a famous cake to remember," she proclaimed. They laughed at the comment of a famous cake. It sounded superficial yet meaningful at the same time. The room went silent at this point. Only the festive tablecloth sounded out in its loud colors. The teacups sat on it with their cheerful shape, and the unfinished curtain hung on a slant, allowing only half the sunlight in. It was shining on Margaret. Her eyes were lit up like a Christmas tree!

Mrs. Roberts opened her mouth, then closed it again. Her heart had something to say, but it took a moment. "I still love Jesus. I still pray, Margaret. I've asked Him to look after you and my son, to marry you both and to have a long life together, to be famous only in His eyes, in what all He has planned. I suppose He used me to help and to support you both. Now I realize He used you to help me too. I think of Jerimiah 29:11, 'For I know the thoughts that I think toward you, says the Lord, thoughts of peace and not of evil, to give you a future and a hope.' It's what I'm still living in belief of for myself, as well as for both of you," she finished saying, then lifted their cups to bring to the sink.

They continued to share the scriptures of Psalms 23 and 24. The twenty-seventh Psalm is the one she read to Margaret, keeping it in her prayers among many others from her Bible, for her and Garth. On Margaret's way home, she thanked the Lord for Mrs. Roberts. When the winding road came to the nasty corner, it revealed its curse but had no power to intimidate anymore. She sang her way through it, and as she drove up to the rough driveway, the car proceeded to bounce her to the house as usual.

Mother must have been in the back with the laundry because she saw shirts fling by and socks fly forward, then backward whenever the line stopped. One time when she brought the dry sheets in, bumblebees came staggering out once they were untangled; you wouldn't see Harriet for the rest of the day because George would trap them in a jar and put them somewhere in her and Margaret's room. Last time they were on her dresser.

"Father, I'm home. I'll help with the milking," she hollered.

"I'm half done. Go help Mother. George can help me," he hollered back.

Mother came to the front yard to find George to help Father with milking. "George, go help your father with the cows. George!" she hollered.

Harriet hollered at everyone, asking why they're hollering. No one answered her because everyone realized they were hollering once she brought it to their attention.

The summer weeks were climbing ahead, and it was time for Father to bring Margaret to her new residence for nursing school. She was excited but still upset that Garth was drafted into the US Army in July. It cut their summer short, and she wasn't sure when she'd see him next.

Being Sunday, she drove to their place to resume plans for the wedding. Margaret always looked forward to quality time with Garth's mother. Together they'd plan, then pray at the end of each visit.

Mrs. Roberts saw her car coiling up the driveway, but this time missing the bump that waits for unsuspecting, or forgetful visitors. Chickens half flying and running at the same time scrambled for their coop. The cows slowly turned their heads with hay clung to their tongues as they made no other movement except for their mouths. There's nothing more perpetual than watching cows eat. Then they want to eat your hair if you get too close. That was a second good reason Margaret wore a shroud while milking.

"Hello, Margaret. Are you ready to begin your nursing career?"

"Yes and no. I have my clothes washed and packed. Got my personal stuff, such as fancy writing paper and my Bible. But I don't know if I'm ready to drive off even though it's not that far from home. I seem to go up and down, strong like a metal bar one minute, then bent as if I was put in a bending press."

"Wow, that is really putting you in a vice of struggles." Mr. Roberts laughed, walking into the house staring at the lopsided curtain once again.

"I have apple squares for you and your father to take on the ride. I made them today," went on Mrs. Roberts. She was studying her husband's reaction to the curtain, knowing how he feels about incomplete jobs and that he'd probably make a smart comment.

"Thank you, we will enjoy that," replied Margaret.

"Well, about the wedding, do you want a sizeable one or small?" asked Mr. Roberts.

"I think it should be big. Garth and I have friends on top of our families."

"I think you both should have a big wedding. I heard that your parents want to announce your engagement in the Binghamton Sun, as well as the Montrose Independent," said Mrs. Roberts.

"Yes, because we still have family and friends in Binghamton, New York. We must send invitations but to just some of them. I'd like a big wedding but not that big. In fact, it may get smaller as we plan if we can't save enough money. I didn't want a small wedding to tell you the truth," she divulged.

"And I'm making the three-tiered cake for you both, so don't worry about that. I saved for it, and it'll be gorgeous," she promised.

"I'm grateful for that and for you. You have been doing more than anyone so far."

She hugged Mr. and Mrs. Roberts and headed to Garth's grandmothers. Garth is expected to call soon, and she's the only one with a phone.

As she opened Grandmother's door, the phone rang out! "Hello, is this you Garth?" asked his grandmother.

"Yes, it's me. Is Margaret with you?" he hurried to say, but before she could answer, she was already handing Margaret the phone.

"Hello, it's me. Are you doing well there? I miss you, honey," she said.

"I am, but it's a lot of training, the kind of work that makes you think hard about home. I miss our Friday nights and you," he said softly.

"Me too. I miss reading our Bibles together opposed to apart, though we always plan to read the same passages. Thanks for poking me to keep reading. I feel guilty if I miss a day or more. I must leave for nursing school in of couple days. I bought stamps for us. I will put some in with my letters to you once I'm settled in. Is there anything else you need such as paper?"

"I just need to hear from you. Can you please be sure to stay in touch?" he asked.

"I will. I'll be busy getting to know everyone there and my schedule, but I promise I'll write," she said.

"Maybe next time we can talk longer if you're not too busy with your nursing. I'm lonely here. I love you, Margaret. It's hard waiting to get married," he genuinely said.

"I will give you a number soon as I can in a letter. I love you too. I miss our walks and talks," she blurted out.

The instant they hung up, Margaret turned to his grandmother for a hug; the Army frightened her.

The drive home was too quiet. All she could think about was if Garth were to be sent into combat in Korea. Right now, he's in Ft. Jackson, South Carolina, for eight weeks of basic training with the 101st Airborne. But they both decided to not worry about it. They left it up to God. Thinking on things is okay but not worrying, she tried to remind herself.

She turned the car off and sat in front of her house. The full effect of going to Johnson City, New York, and the ways of war came flooding in, and "Korea broke the dam."

CHAPTER 6

From Adventure to Illness
to Engagement

It was storming as they drove into Johnson City. The trees were swaying wildly. Branches were barely holding onto their leaves. The wind chased the flowers into one another that once stood in perfect rows, then whipped their heads around. Rain the size of blotches beat at the windshield, splashing outward once they hit. Margaret peered through the window to look for a directional sign leading to the hospital where she would be staying. The streets were bare except for the loose litter that curled around poles and splatted against fences.

"What a greeting this is," Margaret said.

"Not much of a welcome, is it?" Father laughed as he pulled into the drenched hospital parking lot. "We're going to have to wait until this rain slows down, or your belongings will be soaked."

"Then we shall eat more of the apple squares from Mrs. Roberts!" she said with a perky voice.

"Did you both get much wedding planning done?"

"We did, but it's hard to decide on the guest list. More family than friends can come, making it hard to pick which friends," she said as she passed him the desert.

"Well, Mother and I saw a few nice wedding dresses in a store window, but the cost is unaffordable," he expressed with heaviness.

"Hey, the rain is ending. We can get my stuff unloaded. Don't worry, Father. It'll all work out somehow," she said reassuringly.

Once Margaret was moved into her room, Father was hugging her goodbye as two students walked in. They were carrying their books and set them on their beds.

"Hello, are you assigned to this room?" one of them asked.

"Yes. I guess this bed without sheets is mine?" asked Margaret.

"Yep. Hope you don't mind sleeping near the door," said the other roommate.

Father couldn't be more ready to leave the room of pink pillows, anatomy pictures on the walls, and physiology books displayed everywhere. It scared him to the door with Margaret following. She reassured him for the second time that things would be fine. Then he left.

It wasn't so bad because he and Mother worked in the same area. They drove the thirty-five miles each way to work and back every day. If Margaret needed something, it was possible for her to have.

The next morning was the first of "free days," meaning the senior students were to show the new students their classrooms and cafeteria. Margaret's roommates, Linda and Marcy, took her through the building until she was exhausted from climbing stairs and peeking into rooms. The cafeteria was the last stop. There they had lunch with two other girls who insisted on giving out a care package of advice. "Never go near room forty-two. Don't ever be late for Mrs. Doleberg's class. Be sure to keep your uniform spotless. Look before you sit down anywhere, and come see us if you want to party," they said simultaneously.

Margaret asked, "What's in room forty-two?"

"It's not for us to know. The door is never unlocked," whispered Linda.

"There must be teaching tools in there," said Margaret, searching her imagination for any other possible idea.

"No, I think ancient people are in there," shared Marcy.

"I believe there's stacks of chocolate in there," reported one of the other girls.

"You would think that. That's all you ever eat! It's under your pillow, in our bathroom, even between your books," stated her roommate.

"Well, this is my last year here, and I'm finding a way into that room. Who's with me?" pleaded Marcy.

"Why don't we just ask the next person we see entering the room?" mentioned Margaret.

"Are you joking? Even the janitor is not allowed in there. I got his set of endless keys once, and that door has no key! We never see anyone go through that door," gasped Marcy.

"Let me know if you girls ever find out what's in there. I'm a bit curious now." Margaret frowned.

The following morning began with Margaret catapulting out of bed. She thought she was late for class, but Linda was up early doing her hair way ahead of time and woke her with a difficult song she was trying to sing.

"Are you always up this early?" asked Margaret.

Before she could answer, a groan interrupted them. Marcy was coming alive under her knitted blankets.

"It takes her hours to fill her face with makeup and her hands with jewelry, and the singing slows her down even more," grumbled Marcy.

"Speaking of jewelry, what kind of ring are you wearing around your neck, Margaret?" Linda asked, lacking no interest.

"It's a class ring, and I'll be getting my engagement ring some months from now. I've been planning my wedding, but every time we settle on a date, it gets changed for various reasons. Right now, all we know is that it looks like May is the month to go with," she replied while holding out her necklace for them to study the contents of her ring.

Linda flung her hand over her mouth in astonishment and the words "you're getting married?" came spewing out from between her fingers. While she was looking for her second breath, Marcy cheered for Margaret saying, "There's two things I want to do in life, and that's to get in room forty-two and go to your wedding. What's your man's name, girl? I need to know how to address you both."

"Garth Roberts," Margaret proudly announced.

After a quick breakfast, the girls went their separate ways for class.

As the weeks carried on, Margaret enjoyed the challenges in her classes. Chemistry was the most appealing to her. Posters and projects were created by the students and presented in the biology class. That was her second favorite subject; it was the artful class.

Some weekends she was able to go home because of her parents working in a factory in the same town. A thirty-five-mile drive home and back again was a blessing. The Sundays that she could be at Garth's grandmother's for his phone calls was a double blessing. Most of her home time was about wedding planning. The date changed again to April from May because it depended on his Army schedule as usual. And now it was going to be a smaller wedding after all.

By the time November ended, Margaret had only been in school three months and was still looking into other classrooms to admire posters. She and Marcy found a set of keys that afternoon, under anatomy pictures on a professor's desk. Room forty-two blared like a siren in Marcy's mind. They stared at one another in disbelief.

"These couldn't be the keys! They're probably just car keys belonging to…" Margaret stopped. Someone was entering the room.

"Do you girls need help in finding the right room because I don't recognize either of you to be my medical students," interjected a tall man with a massive beard who entered from across his room. Marcy recovered the keys from nearly slipping out of her trembling hand while his eyes were on Margaret.

"We were wondering what the medical students' biology classroom looked like," said a nervous Margaret.

"We love biology," added Marcy.

"If you two leave right now, I won't say anything to your biology professor. I'll leave you to your professor, and you can leave my students to me," he growled.

"We are sorry," Margaret said as they turned to leave, his eyes trailing after them.

Margaret felt paralyzed. Her heart was riddled with fear, and the nerves in her throat jumped around like a grasshopper.

"I'm going to our room to do homework," said a relieved Margaret after a fast-paced walk down the hall.

"After all this time, I finally have keys to try, and you want to do homework. If you like a challenge in your classes, what do you think this is?" bragged Marcy.

"Very well then, I'll come with you, but I won't go in if a key opens the door. I'll stand in the hall and keep watch. You can tell me what's in there afterward," she said, making it obvious to Marcy that she wanted no more trouble.

At the turn of the second key tried, the door popped open. Marcy scrambled inside but didn't get far. The room was pitch black and screamed with silence. Not one window provided daylight because there were no windows! The light switch wasn't even near the door. She crept around, feeling the wall for a positive outcome.

Margaret couldn't stand the waiting. She paced the hall, then slipped into the black silence, closing the door behind her. Putting her thoughts on hold, she whispered to Marcy, but no sound came back. Margaret seldom got into a sketchy situation like or unlike this and felt overcome with the thickness of darkness.

Suddenly light flared throughout the room by itself, filling unfamiliar pickling jars with a yellowish glow of incandescent lighting! Both girls stood alarmed at the sight that confined them to their spot, tiny faces of floating animals were looking at them through a series of sealed jars. A dissecting table with tools rolled in cloth were on standby. Other things that they weren't sure of sat on shelves.

"Marcy, this is the medical professor's study room. This must be what his students do in the conjoined room through that door over by you," she declared.

"Wow, I knew he was strange, but there needs to be a better place to store these specimens. He has about as much charm as that, whatever that is in that jar in front of you," she said with hesitance.

"I never wanted to come in here. Besides, we aren't supposed to be in this room in the first place, remember? It serves us right that we are having an appalling day," Margaret proclaimed.

"Hey, I am not your big sister in nursing for nothing. I was assigned to you, and I'll take responsibility if anyone finds out we were digging around in a creepy room full of pickled mummies. Let's get back to our room and tell Linda our grisly discovery. She'll wish she hadn't missed out. I'll never look at that medical professor the same again, not that I want to look at him at all," whispered Marcy. Margret figured this was going to be an intriguing year if it continues with these roommates. She wasn't expecting adventure along with her studies, at least not of the mischief type.

The last day of the week came, and Margaret went home to report how it went. Harriet's emotions spilled out, convincing her older sister that she was missed. She was closing in on the age of fifteen, qualifying her to have many assorted feelings which tipped the scales in their home, and too many for Father to identify with. He put Mother in charge of his second daughter and investigated George instead. George had been experimenting with cigarettes, but they found out before he was snared by the crave for them. Furthermore, Margie was busy that weekend, therefore leaving Margaret to wonder about when they'd pick up from where they left off. She'd have to save her secret room story for later too.

With December suddenly barreling in, she and Garth were writing each other several letters; usually two a week, plus phone calls on one Sunday a month, when she could be at his grandmother's. Mrs. Roberts compiled a list of their family and friends, including Margaret's, for the wedding invitations. The list was growing into a mob of guests. Surely they would have to review it; otherwise, some would go hungry. At least she had their cake under control. The wedding dress was up in the air though. It seemed everything but the dress had much of their focus, yet Margaret wasn't worried. She knew Jesus was miraculous when it came to weddings! He declared His deity of purity, preservation, and restoration in his first miracle by turning simple water into fresh grape juice; and the king said it was the best wine saved for last! He bypassed the steps in making it by not cleaning the used pots, He reused them, which wasn't a custom to do. He didn't press the grapes, and He didn't make new pots of stone. The miracle was in the water; it was pure, not defiled (John 2:1–10). If Jesus can make fresh grape juice out of thin air, He can make a wedding dress appear too, she believed.

December proved to be a difficult month for Margaret. There were less bizarre adventures in the hospital and more in her books as they carried her deeper into anatomy followed by the lab projects. The medical room of swimming faces and organs swiftly shot to her memory every time she turned a page or looked at a poster. But her classes weren't the real problem. She didn't feel well. Staying awake had become a chore in class. She'd find herself nodding off during her favorite subject. Most of the month was characterizing her as an uninterested and careless student.

The next time Margaret was home, she went to see her doctor. He informed her that she had mono, a viral infection that makes the patient extremely tired. It can last several weeks or months depending on the health of the immune system she was told. Her health must have been compromised with the pressure of school, the wedding, and the fact that mother needed surgery. She needed one for a hiatal hernia with the possibility of a second one for gallstones. There would be virtually nobody but Harriet and George to help Father on the farm. They could perhaps get into trouble, giving Father a heavier load to manage, she acknowledged.

By the end of the third week in December, Margaret's classes were winding down to a halt. Christmas would soon be on the doorstep, with the world pausing for the Savior's birthday! It was always a blessed holiday, but sadness would accompany gladness for her this year.

The bad news came in a meeting with two of Margaret's professors from her nursing program. They suggested she think about becoming a practical nurse instead of a registered nurse because her marks were falling below the school's standard.

"I haven't been well for some time," claimed Margaret. "I've been diagnosed with mono by my doctor back home."

"We see how that could affect your outcome, but it's too late to go back with the other students who will be moving forward after the holidays. Their last big group project for my biology class has been handed in. They couldn't put your name on it because you missed your part in the project," explained one of the professors. However, the chemistry professor would have liked to see Margaret succeed but knew it wasn't plausible with all the work she missed in her class as well.

Mother was totally incredulous about Margaret's bad news. She believed she should go back after Christmas and try again. Father's heart hurt over it. He knew she could have been the town's nurse had she not fallen ill. The record will always stand as "she would have finished her degree but was unable to for a different reason than that of incompetents."

Christmas was exciting! Garth was home, and despite Margaret's career change from nursing to possibly working at IBM or EJ's, she kept persevering. Garth wanted her to work at IBM, but she would probably end up at EJ's shoe factory because they were hiring, and it was easy to get on there. And that's exactly what happened after Christmas; the saying "a girl can never have enough shoes" must have come from factories such as this one, supposed Margaret.

Garth bought her a leather purse for Christmas which was a nice surprise, and a girl can never have too many of those either. It replaced her current one that went into storage at the top of her closet. It wasn't much of a purse anyway. Her new one meant so much more seeing as it was from him and his good taste.

Dinner was awesome because as usual, Father was the cook. Harriet considered Margaret as her gift since she missed her terribly when she was in nursing. George was beginning to wonder what Christmas was all about. He and Harriet still considered what their parents and sister believed but weren't ready to take the next step. Mother was not well. Her surgery wasn't until March, making it difficult to put up with the side effects of her hernia and gallstones.

The year is about to turn to 1956 with their wedding just four months away. It took many letters to plan for the right month and day. Over the last year, those letters proved their devotion to one another, not to mention their hopes for the Army to be more forgiving in their future; they consider newly married men! Once they get married, she'd be almost thirteen hundred miles from home yet still not knowing what to expect in Army life. Mother and Father felt it would be a strain on their new marriage, but really, it would be more of a strain on them. They were still preparing in conditioning themselves for the inevitable wedding. However, they were cordial with Garth and his parents, but it would take some time before they truly accepted everything. On the other hand, his parents and grandmother being close with Margaret and the idea of marriage was welcomed from the beginning.

Christmas holidaying was lovely with the snow gently falling around the favorite couple in Little Meadows. Icicles draped in different lengths from rooftops, collecting light from the distant sun that revealed the cracks in their structure. Once again, Margaret used her education to explain how this formation works. She understood the periodic table of the elements and the chemistry behind the everyday organic and inorganic reactions. But it always amazed her that not one snowflake or icicle was even nearly alike. In her mind, God was not only an author, painter, and Creator but a designer with everything proportionally done without a drawing board.

Margaret spent time exchanging wedding ideas with Garth in the one week that he was home. Everyone had a part in either the wedding or the planning. Arrangements began, then were put on hold because the date and time never stood secured long enough to do the invitations. Just when a date was set, it flipped to a different month and day. Margaret was beginning to see the bouncing effects of Army life.

"My week is up, Margaret. This past 168 hours was the most normal I've had in a long time," swallowed Garth.

"Me too, but not as unprivileged as your time in the Army. I had and still have our families near me. Did I tell you how much money I saved toward our wedding?" she sputtered, trying to change the subject because tears were swelling in her eyes.

"Yes, you did. We have, I guess I can't exactly remember now, but I know it's enough for some of what we need. You spoke about it covering the invitations maybe my ring, gas for the Ford if it's in running condition, and a cabin to stay at for a couple days if it works out that way," he said, still trying to remember what else.

"Yes, I really like the cabin idea. Right now, I'm saving for Harriet's dress, one dress to save for at a time, I guess. Hopefully we have success when we go shopping. Margie has moved away and will not be able to attend our wedding. It's sad because she was my closest friend throughout school. We always thought we would see each other get married. Your mom says she's still making our cake," she added, with her tears holding to her eyelids as long as they could, then dropping to the frozen ground.

The day ended with each of them clutched to their Bibles for spiritual reinforcement. The power and will of God were enough to bind them even though soon 1,200–1,300 miles would separate them again.

The next couple of months dragged on, and Mother was preparing for her doctor appointment early one morning. Today would conclude when, why, and what if for her.

Margaret was overwhelmed one day, then overjoyed the next! The day and month of March was ousted, with April as the replacement. Her and Garth's letters were coming from opposite directions to meet in the middle of wedding talk. Needing to pick a day in April was one of the issues. Between the date and the groom's outfit, neither was decided on just yet but was inching closer. She found herself tossing colors around in her head only to finally let him pick if he wanted to wear a suit in blue or brown or his uniform.

"I'm home. I need to speak with everyone," called Mother. The screen door didn't split the silence this time. It creaked its way to the frame instead. Father was holding it back from slamming against it.

"What's wrong, Father?" Margaret asked, observing their motionless faces.

"Mother needs to lay down because the ride home wasn't a warm or smooth one. She'll be having surgery in March after all. That'll be about three weeks and two days from now," he reported.

"We'll all help with the farm chores and housework," said Margaret. George and Harriet nodded their heads in agreement.

"Not a pleasant thing to be told on Valentine's Day, Mother. I'm sorry about you spending it this way, but we do have a card and a stick of chocolate for you," she said, then smiled.

"Thank you, Margaret. I will enjoy the card more than the chocolate though. It'll upset my gallstones," she said.

George hoped Mother would give him the chocolate, but Harriet held out her hand first.

At that moment, Margaret captured a figure swooping past the kitchen window. It ducked down, then popped upright again. It was the mailman, now stepping in full view to rap on the door.

"Here's your package, Margaret. I need you to sign for it," he instructed, then proceeded to rattle off down the driveway in his 1937 Chevy.

"Oh, it can't be…it is…it must be," she gushed, as she crept into the kitchen, keeping the door from slamming shut behind her, then rustled through the junk drawer to get the scissors. The package was wrapped and tied as though the contents may escape. Nothing was able to open it but scissors. She snuck to her bedroom, slipping by the others who were making Mother comfortable in her and Father's room.

At last, the braided strings gave in to her weapon, revealing the shredded wrapping on her lap and a shiny rock. February fourteenth was one like no other. Margaret whirled herself onto her bed with her feet pointed out and her hand floating in midair. The transformation of a girl into an engaged girl filled the room with majestic moments of the reality that lay ahead.

That night, she slept in a glorious state. Dreams of a heavenly wedding and diamonds passed through her suspended consciousness. Decorated horses hitched to an embellished chariot carried her and her groom into a mist that, upon exiting, revealed a field of summer flowers. A waterfall of gold dust poured alongside it. The snow-white horses drifted along the edge, then stood like royalty while they picked a bouquet of flowers and ran their hands through the sparkling cascading dust. Jesus appeared to them, beckoning them, and they stepped forward into marriage.

CHAPTER 7

She's in My Dress!

The morning sun grazed over Margaret's hand. As she came to, she jolted herself into a sitting position, searching her hand for the diamond ring. It sprayed with colors in the sunlight while she tipped it in different directions. Next, she collected some pretty paper and a pen to write a letter.

Dearest Garth (genuine letter):

I got your letter and package. Oh, honey, I can't say what's on my heart; there isn't words for it. The ring is beautiful! I love it and the one who sent it. You don't have to worry about me wearing and being proud of it. I'm proud to wear it and show everyone that I belong to you and our love for one another. It was the nicest Valentines you could have sent. I woke up this morning, and first thing I did was to look and see if that "rock" was still on the finger of my left hand. It fits perfect. Couldn't be better. Oh, honey, I love you so. I wish I could tell you in person. Pen and ink do such a poor job of it.

Last night, Mrs. Condon and Andy were over. Mrs. Condon came over to help with the quilt, though she was quite curious as to why the mailman came up to the house. They never miss a trick. Andy was teasing me about getting it from the mailman.

I was so excited when it came that I could hardly sign for it. Then I couldn't get it opened. Boy! That string and tape sure didn't want to come off!

I wanted the family to notice it by themselves, so I didn't say anything. Harriet was first. She saw it while I was cutting onions at the stove. I told her not to say anything to Mom and Dad, to let them find out. Mom didn't notice it. She asked if the package came, so I showed her. Then when Dad came in, she told him. George never found out until almost after supper. Then Harriet asked him if he had looked at my left hand. Poor George. He sure is baffled by the goings on. He didn't say much for a while. Then Condon came; he took charge and had to show it off.

Guess I'll stop here for now. I'll write more in the morning. I love you, darling. More than tongue can tell.

All my love, Margaret.

Margaret spent the entire day to herself other than heckling with the chickens on the front step that morning in order to get through them to get to the barn. Father had been expecting her to begin draining her share of cows.

As the day slowly vanished, the nightly stars stretched out against the darkened sky. Some grouped together, and others were strewn like whitish-blue Christmas lights hanging from nothing. Margaret came in from star gazing to talk with Mother and Father before bed. Mother looked tired and wilted. "I want you both to know that I'll never be as happy as I am now. Garth makes me want to study my Bible more because we share Scripture in our letters. He always tells me in his letters that I need to keep praying and trust the Lord in everything. We share sermons from Sunday over 1,200 miles away, 1,200 miles," she repeated.

"He has been growing in the Lord," admitted Father.

"Yes, I have written him letters, and I detected a genuine response from him again and again," recounted mother.

"I believe you deserve a chance to be happy, seeing as you've expressed that in one way or another nearly every day for the past few years," Father noted.

"Another thing, I need to be out of the hospital and on my feet before the wedding. I may not be perfectly pleased about it, but I'm not missing out on father walking you down the aisle," Mother pointed out.

"I don't know what else I can say, Mother, except that I know it's God's will for me and Garth to join together as one," she reasoned.

Father broke through the strained moment of silence to ask Margaret about her engagement gift that Garth's brother built for her. "I heard you filled your hope chest already," he mentioned.

"I've been adding things since February. However, I can squeeze more in yet. Donald did a lovely job of it. I told him its just what I hoped for. I'm glad he's going to be a part of the wedding," she added.

George came into the room clouding the atmosphere with his irritableness, then pulled himself up the stairs by the railing. He didn't know what part he would have in the wedding and was too bored to ask. He tripped and fell on the stairs, lying there until he became bored enough with his boredom to pick himself up. He was feeling as though he was going to become extinct with everyone engaged in talk about the wedding every day. Even the barn animals lost interest in him. Every time he tried to talk to the chickens, they tilted their heads to the side to glare at him from one eyeball. And the rooster used to be more dependent upon him but now has a new persona. He's got class and is popular with the chicks!

March fourth came in on the horizon with the sun peeking over the hills before rising to its fullness in brilliance. The land was serene until Margaret sprung out of bed, scaring the early birds off the windowsill, putting an end to the silence. Immediately they came back to peek through the window, chirping at her in disapproval of being spooked like that. She laughed at the fact that they turned themselves into angry balls of ruffled feathers as she climbed into her housecoat and flipped her slippers over to sit upright. She placed her feet inside, then strolled down to make breakfast. No further performances were activated on the staircase seeing as her wedding was a reality now!

George, Harriet, and Father were assembled in the stable milking the cows. Margaret was running the house like a conveyer belt while Mother stayed off her feet. She timed the bacon to the chores, and ran out to hang laundry, then got dressed, plus kicked the clucking chickens off the step from crowding at the door. They continually pecked at the bits of fallen seeds under the bird feeder, but it was a gentle kick thanks to the sweet soul God engraved in her. "I'm highest in the pecking order here, so better remember that, you chicken chickens." She laughed.

Mother, now standing at her bedroom door, shook her head at the woman before her that still had a child's heart at times.

"I'm headed for shopping, Mother. I'll cook the eggs first, then call the others in to eat. I have a mountain of things to shop for to do with my wedding," she insisted.

"Don't forget your list," called Mother.

"I think it's in my purse," she said, confirming it while admiring the youthful appearance of it. It was certainly for her age. Garth was a sharp shopper; however, so was she. Today would prove it! "Harriet, we have to leave now. I'll be waiting in the car. Time is essential," she emphasized. "Praise God, the car is fixed so I can shop. Praise God for Garth. Praise God for keeping us safe," she conceded aloud, granting God acknowledgment of His involvement in her life. "I'm sorry, Lord, that I've been using the excuse of being too busy to read my Bible, so I brought it along on the trip to read a passage before I shop. I believe You want this marriage to take place. Will You choose the right wedding gown for me, Lord?" she asked, with her hands folded in prayer.

They picked up Shirley on the way, and upon parking the car at their destination, Margaret opened her Bible to read about God's guidance while the other two jumped out, dodging the curb with their shopping energy that nearly landed them in a pile of slush. Harriet laughed with Shirley about their eagerness to shop.

Moments later, something urged Margaret to slowly lift her unsuspecting eyes to a most glamorous sight. It stood right in front of her in the display window, a mannequin soaked in satin and lace with a veil to its waist.

"She's in my dress," came a soft voice from Margaret. She moved herself out of the car, barely closing the door. Awareness of streets and people bustling in all directions around her failed to exist. Recognition of multiple sounds couldn't be heard as a result of the floating dress drowning them out. "It's like my dream," she whispered. Unable to move from the spot at the window, Harriet tugged at her arm to bring her back from the heavenly garment.

"You better get in there and snap up that dress, Margaret. You know it's the month most girls go hunting for a wedding dress after capturing a man over winter. Some get married on simple promises of 'to love and to adore for life,'" cautioned Shirley.

"Yeah, until they turn wrinkly and start burning supper often," joked Harriet.

"My man will love my wrinkles, including my cooking. He's unlike other men, Harriet. He's like Dad in that way," insisted Margaret.

"Enough! Let's get that dress," ordered Harriet.

The clerk opened the door to the three arrivals on his doorstep. "You girls have been standing outside looking at the charming wedding dresses," he said while observing their expressions to see which one was possibly getting married.

"I would like to try on the one in the middle of your showcase of satin and lace. It's what I'm looking for," Margaret announced.

"Well, it's the last one I have like that. Not sure if it'll fit, I was thinking of keeping it in the widow to inspire shoppers," he blubbered, hinting at the other dresses with his body language. He tried to divert Margaret's eyes to them, but she had eyes for the middle one only.

"You mean to inspire the thought of marriage to young pass-ersby," Harriet playfully suggested.

He didn't answer her and agreed to pull the dress from the mannequin that Margaret asked for. Harriet took it upon herself to redress the stiff humanlike doll with a coat, tying it around her funny body. She included a bonnet for good measure, then stood back to see how impressive it looked while the clerk assisted her sister with shoes. She spotted gloves on a nearby table and jammed one on the doll's hand only to break off its finger.

"Harriet, you fractured her finger," Shirley said, concealing her voice so no one would hear.

Harriet knew she had better conceive of a plan to reconnect it before the clerk discovers her body without it.

"Put the finger in the glove first. Then slip it over the hand. It'll hold it on until someone changes her outfit. They'll think it broke while undressing her," whispered Shirley.

Harriet panicked to get the glove on, breaking off two more fingers! "Oh, God, if you're there, help me. I am beyond desperate to fix this brittle doll," she pleaded.

Just then, the clerk stepped up beside her. He was astonished at his incomplete mannequin. Harriet handed him the glove half full of fingers. When he reached for it, he knocked the thumb from his brand-new mannequin. Harriet asked if he'd like her to add it to the glove! His eyeballs grew dark and narrowed. Harriet folded her lips inward before they broke into a smile. You could have heard a pin drop until a noise came from the dressing room.

Margaret unknowing what was playing out between the others stood in a dreamlike state in the mirror, looking better than the gal in the window, she figured. If she only knew how much better. At least she had all her fingers, especially her wedding ring finger!

She stepped out from the dressing room to look at three seri-ous faces that suddenly changed from bent eyebrows to raised ones. Harriet had mischievousness written all over hers.

"Margaret, you look splendid," exclaimed Harriet.

"Unbelievably beautiful in that gown and veil. Wait until Garth sees you coming down the aisle," cheered Shirley.

The clerk was fascinated at how the gown took on life with a real person in it.

"You spell gorgeous in that dress Margaret," remarked Shirley.

"It's the one I must get. I won't find one nearly like it," stressed Margaret.

"How much is it? Mom will think it's too fancy. Didn't Dad say to not pay too much?" pried Harriet.

"It's enough to thin out my savings, still, I'm buying it," rejoiced the bride-to-be. While paying for it with her and Garth's savings, the clerk added the cost of the fractured fingers, feeling a bit shameful knowing that she didn't know exactly why. The girls spilled out in laughter over the incident, filling Margaret in as they tilled their way through the slush to get to the car.

"Well, I hope other places are on your list, Margaret. Are we shopping for our dresses somewhere else on the grounds that there weren't hardly any in that store? I'm a bit worried we may not do as well as you did today," said Shirley.

"I know where we can go. It's at the other end of town. Mother told me that she spotted dresses there for bridesmaids," said Margaret with encouragement.

"I hope the mannequins there are made of something sturdier than the last one. That last one was a poor creation," Harriet giggled.

"Well, you weren't supposed to be dressing it," chirped Margaret.

"But I couldn't just leave it the way it was in the window for all to see. It would stick in the minds of everyone going by. It's face and neck were nice enough, but underneath, it was horribly made. The coat was its only hope," decided Harriet.

"Okay, we're here. Let's see what we can find," interrupted Shirley.

The girls explored the large store and found the perfect dresses for the wedding. They had to order them and were informed that thankfully, they would be in on time.

"It's too bad Sharon couldn't have been with us to pick out her dress, but it is best she orders it with you, Margaret," cautioned Shirley.

"I know she wanted a dress in violet which I agreed to, but not sure on choosing the shade. I'll go with her on Saturday to decide," said Margaret.

Once Shirley was home, Margaret and Harriet had a sister-to-sister discussion as night was about to fall around them on their way home. With concern, they discussed how life is going to shift for the family without Margaret once she's married and transported over 1,200 miles away. They agreed on the fact that everyone will have to get used to her being gone.

Margaret swept up her gown from the back seat into her arms and ran upstairs to bury herself in its satin and lace, trim and all. The depth of night drew out the stars from their hiding places, sprinkling them near and far. They resembled dancing dots from out her window. Two were blinking at her, compelling her to wish upon them, not that she believed in such things. One trickled across the well-dressed sky, then fell with a striking light through the darkness as she laid sleeping in the arms of God.

As morning dawned, the sun took shape and plastered its light onto their bedroom walls. Margaret realized she slept next to her dress the entire night.

"Margaret, you're supposed to wear it, not sleep with it." Harriet frowned, who was already dressed for chores.

"Never mind that. I was going to sleep in it." Margaret chuckled.

"I'm going to write Garth to tell him your wedding dress will be well used by the time he sees it."

"No, you won't since he'll receive my letter first, talking about your silly letter. It seems to me that my letter will have preference over yours," she said, relishing the idea of him standing on her side now and always. "In all seriousness, Harriet, will you help George and Father with the milking? I really do need to write Garth to tell him about our shopping adventure."

"All right, I'll tell them they have me instead of you today. They won't like it 'cause I'm real slow. I milk every minute I can on just one cow, get it?" she said, twisting her mouth with laughter.

"No, I don't, but thanks anyway," teased Margaret.

Dearest Garth (genuine sections of letter):

Well honey, I've changed my mind again about what kind of wedding it will be, but this time for good. I got my gown yesterday. I started out to buy a nice white dress and ended up with a beautiful lace and satin wedding gown. Also, we picked out the bridesmaids' gowns: turquoise (blue green) for Shirley, yellow for Harriet, and violet for Sharon. Harriet and Shirley were with me, so theirs are ordered. I guess we'll go up next Saturday and have Sharon order hers. My mother is going into the hospital Friday, so that's why I wanted to get everything settled… Just think, honey, only two more months!

Your dad was telling me about the Ford. He said there was no use in you getting in debt when the Ford was in good shape. He just had some more work done on it this last week. Boy, hon, it will be swell to have our "old Ford." To me, it seems to be a part of us and our good times of the past and future. I kind of hated the thought of giving it up…

Mom and dad would like us to stay here. They even said they would save the front bedroom for us and in our family, that is an honor! That bedroom has always been for company. All the years we've lived in this house, none of us kids have ever slept there.

Though with all this excitement, I'm worried about mom. She probably won't be out of the hospital until the end of the month…

Honey, I'm not going to worry about things. The Lord will see that we have everything we need. Look at how He worked out the car. We

have a good car and didn't have to borrow a cent.
If we can only remember that all through life!
The Lord will take care of His own.

Boy, it's been just like spring out today. So
nice and warm and sunshiny. I didn't go out but
would have liked to.

Boy, now I'm going to miss you more than
ever. Remember how we always went for walks
on Sunday afternoons? Oh well, it won't be long
now. Guess I better close. I'll write again as soon
as I can and give you a briefing on the services.

God bless and keep you.

Love, Margaret.

It was incomparable joy from chores when Margaret cooked
up breakfast. She certainly built up enough practice to run her own
kitchen or a farm for that matter. "One day, they won't make farm
girls like they used to" is what the old people have been saying for
years. "Margaret's a good look'n', farm cook'n' girl" is what her dad
commonly says.

At that moment, the screen door slammed three times with
George the last to come in. The chickens darted in different directions and met up again under the bird feeder above the stairs. He
scrambled out of his boots when he smelled the pancakes that were
waiting on the hot plate.

Mother was feeling a little better, good enough to finally decorate her mind with wedding ideas. It was perfect timing because
Margaret was on her way downstairs to show off her wedding gown.
It would be her last time to portray herself as an engaged woman to
be married, but without pretending. Yet the stairs looked up at her,
waiting for her to mount her first step into the world of acting. The
handrail once again lent itself for its famous part in the script. She
clutched it with one hand and lifted the gown with the other. With
each step, she felt numb yet alive, small yet magnified, young yet
mature, single yet married.

Once the family all sat down, she embellished herself before them, spinning around to model it.

"Margaret, its lovely," cried Mother.

"I saw it first, and Shirley told her to snap it up before any other girls could spot it," divulged Harriet.

"I knew it was the one before I got out of the car," said Margaret.

"I saw the pancakes first and would like to snap one up before someone else spots them," protested George.

"Sorry, George, I got carried away," admitted Margaret.

"Yeah, over 1,200 miles away," cringed George.

Nobody said a word after George dumped his latest and greatest emotion. Margaret flopped her gown onto the couch and straightened out her nightgown, then served the pancakes. She handed him the syrup and butter, now knowing how he felt about the last seven confusing months of nursing, not nursing, and plans to wed. He later decided to join the club and send Garth another letter of his recognition of him becoming a family member.

Mother piped up to declare her version of Margaret's up and coming big day. She rolled out one idea after the other. Father thought she was either losing her mind or found it, considering she fought with her own emotions for a long time about who her daughter should spend her life with. Maybe God convinced her to simply love her kids, not own them. Maybe she gave Him the reins after all, he silently hoped.

April turned the corner, making itself the most memorable one of the twelve calendared months. Corresponding through more letters, they closed in on the wedding day of the twenty eighth. It was the eighteenth, then the twenty first, and before that, different months of sorted days. The flurry that jailed Margaret's mind from an absolute day broke forth in surety. Margaret thought it kind of compares to an unbeliever sitting in darkness until his coming to Christ frees him to see the light.

Next Saturday came for Margaret to go shopping with Sharon. They picked the maid of honor dress in violet of a light bluish-purple and ordered it.

"I haven't seen your wedding gown, Margaret, but Shirley told me all about it. I can't believe it went from shopping for a nice white dress to an actual wedding dress. And satin smothered in lace was least expected. I'm excited for you. When is Garth coming back?" she added as they plugged along the drenched roads of April.

"He's back on the twenty fourth. I told him that I purchased my dress and lightly described it, but it's not the same as seeing it. So I don't imagine I gave too much away. I can't believe it either, there it hung before me, dangling from a doll. Did Shirley tell you about the mannequin?"

"Oh wow, yes, that was hilarious. You shouldn't have had to pay for her fingers though. I suspect the clerk was just going to glue them on his dummy anyway. Then again, she'll have to wear gloves, permanently." Sharon laughed.

"I definitely have a mountain of stories to share with Garth since he was last here, but he may not appreciate the one about Mrs. Condon following me around to find out what was in my parcel I received. Her son, Andy, came over with her afterward, and he teased me about getting my ring from the mailman. His husky laughter filled the house with thunder, echoing in Mother's head. However, I did put just him in my last letter instead of waiting to tell him about it in person," she noted.

"Good idea. Thanks for asking me to be your maid of honor. You're going to have a glorious day. We all will!" promised Sharon.

"Yes, but more planning yet due to what the men will be wearing. I'm leaving it up to Garth if he wants to wear a suit of his color choice or his uniform. I might be looking at a uniform from the other end of the aisle," suggested Margaret.

"Well, you know what they say 'bout a man in a uniform. Some look pretty sharp!" admitted Sharon.

"Garth looks sharp in everything," confessed Margaret as they pulled into her driveway. "I'll let you know when the dresses arrive. We three will get together to install our opinions and inspirations, never know, perhaps we may want to confuse everyone by me wearing a white shoe and a purple shoe!" Margaret giggled.

"That would be bizarre. Can you imagine having to digest that every time you looked at your wedding pictures?" Sharon shuddered as they began to laugh uncontrollably.

"Thanks for a fun day. I'm positive we'll all love the outcome. See you soon for inspection day." Margaret smiled.

On the remaining miles home, she thanked God for laughter, encouraging friends like Sharon, and the fitting husband-to-be, no matter what he wears!

CHAPTER 8

The Morning Bride

It's April twenty-fifth. Ten inches of snow filled the fields one last time and burdened everyone by obstructing their plans for spring, including the plan for Margaret to see Garth. They were locked in their houses watching the snow drifts piling higher. Remaining stooks from last fall caved under unlimited snowfalls and blizzards in winter, and now a spring blizzard is pounding them again. The good news is that they weren't collected because last summer produced plenty of hay in the countryside. Margaret cleared off the front stairs, making way for the door to move back and forth, then filled the snowy bird feeder. It looked like Christmas, plus with the wedding a few days away, it felt like it.

Mother had her operation in March and was home but somewhat bedridden like before she went in. Her wondering thoughts were climbing the walls of her mind in fear of the wedding taking place without her.

"Margaret, you did send off all the invitations, right?" called Mother

"Yes, I did that with Mrs. Roberts awhile ago. I think I have covered everything," she assured Mother while putting away the breakfast dishes.

"Is George's suit ready? Is Father's suit ready?" echoed Mother.

"No, Mother," she hesitated, then continued, "they're squirreled away in the attic since neither of them fit."

"Are you trying to make me laugh or scream? If I do either, I'll be in bed longer."

"Sorry, I'm just in a healthy mood. Three days and I'll be identifying with all married women. I didn't know I'd be hauling a load of emotions. Nevertheless, I have identified them, and the only one that I sort of object to is my nervousness of the limelight. I'm not one for spotlights, though it is perfectly right for a bride to take center stage," supposed Margaret.

"It's not like you'll be alone in the spotlight," sympathized Mother.

"You said it, Mom! And I'll never feel alone again for as long as I live," she declared.

The twenty-seventh brought Garth and Margaret together, traveling up and down the glassy roads to visit with each set of parents before the following day of the wedding.

"It looks a lot like the arctic out here. The land appears to be one huge, feathered blanket," Margaret suddenly said, breaking the silence.

"It also resembles bundled cotton on branches. I wonder if there will be a clear sky later tonight," he added.

"All this time of planning together by letters and a phone call one Sunday a month has taught me to never take marriage for granted," commented Margaret.

"I agree. Hey, we're here, and look! I can see my mom peering out the window. She always waits for me, just like your mom waits for you," he said with a thoughtful smile.

"Sometimes I think she's as excited for us as we are." She laughed.

"Well, my parents love you. They also know that our relationship hasn't consisted of anything but talking and hugging with a kiss goodbye. I'm proud of us for that reason," he pointed out.

"And that's one thing my parents can attest to after all the times Mom encouraged Dad to peek in the barn. He went back to report on how we sat with our Bibles, engaged in discussion. I'm proud too," she concluded.

"God is our witness. We kept Him before us for a long time and will again tonight. I believe we've been transparent," he boasted, with sincerity.

They climbed out of the car to meet his mom at the door. Mr. Roberts was waiting inside.

"Hello, everyone," beamed Margaret.

"How's the little bride doing?" challenged Mr. Roberts, knowing that Margaret was taming her excitement as best she could.

"I'm doing well. Don't know if I'll sleep all that good tonight though. My heart keeps sinking, then floats up again," replied Margaret as she rooted herself into the soft couch.

"Now don't let Mr. Roberts make it worse," forewarned Mrs. Roberts.

"I'm not about to do anything to her. I'm pleased that your heart finds its right spot again, Margaret," he joked.

Margaret grinned at him, then turned to Garth as he sat down next to her. His mom brought out a plate of sliced apples and cheese with tea to make it an official visit. They proceeded to debate the meaning of marriage by rolling out the red-carpet words, only to roll some of them back in again.

"Look, marriage is about adapting, compensating, promoting, investing, and communicating," specified his mom.

"Sometimes it's about processing, dodging, surviving, and later, assessing the damage. Margaret, you're getting a rolling pin for a wedding present, the one she used on me!" bellowed Mr. Roberts.

With a piece of cheese frozen between Margaret's fingers, she stared at them, unable to put it in her mouth. If she laughed, it would mean she likes the gift idea of a rolling pin. If she didn't laugh, she thought they'd think that she thinks they're easily hostile over disagreements. She plunked the cheese in her mouth in order to say nothing at all.

"Thanks for the advice. We'll think about those words when we think of you both," uttered Garth.

"I believe your words will become mine, Mother," Margaret quietly said.

Hearing that, Mrs. Roberts looked up to acknowledge the face of a girl she would seriously miss. "Margaret, I have something for you. Come with me for a moment." She motioned, with her hand. They entered her bedroom to see a box on the bed. "I want you to have this when you walk down that aisle. Everyone will marvel, but more importantly, you will be pleasing God. You decorate it how you want with some of these," she said.

"This matches my gown. I love it. Thank you for the last four years too. It's difficult to move so far away from the support I'm used to having here. I'll miss you and Mr. Roberts. You're like second parents to me," she told her.

"Margaret, we better leave for your place. Your parents will be expecting us for the visit they planned," reminded Garth.

"I'm ready to go," she said, then stepped under his mom and dad's wings of love for a hug.

They drove along, discussing what leaving for their new life might be like being far from home. His letters told her what it was like to be alone, "You're scared to be scared because you must always keep your head." She would not feel as isolated as he did by having nothing but letters for emotional survival.

The visit would go well with her parents. He had her home by eight as was requested. He never objected to their wishes, only to being held responsible for what wasn't in his control; no one chooses their family, God does, and others often forget that! The thief on the cross may not have been pleasing to his wife's family either, if he had a wife, but Jesus saved him the same as He can save anyone.

The food tray was handed around, and the red-carpet words were rolled out.

"What's the most important thing to remember in marriage?" they asked.

Margaret raised her eyebrows implying she knew the answer to that. "You have to adapt, compensate, promote, invest, and communicate," she promptly said.

"And we already have the rolling pin," Garth added.

"Rolling pin?" asked Mother.

"Yes, in case the communication fails." Garth chuckled.

With that said, Father burst out into laughter. Mother was alarmed until she realized she was the only serious one in the room. Their lightheartedness provoked her to at least smile.

George and Harriet came to see what the fun was though it had ended on a confusing note due to the look on Mother's face. George appeared bewildered as so many times before.

"Harriet, I hope your dress is still hanging," pestered Mother.

"It's hanging by its neckline and not a wrinkle in it," she reported.

"That sounds lethal," said George.

"That was the intention," replied Harriet.

The evening included Harriet's sauciness, which was expected. It was her way of dealing with life's changes yet keeping it fun.

"Let's look at some Scripture before you have to leave, Garth," suggested Margaret's father.

Every time the Bible is brought out, it turns from darkness to daylight in the world of relationships and acceptance. Margaret was thinking it was by reason of Christ's power to ingrain the fundamental truth of family; to reject another true Christian would be to go against the family God created through ingrafting the Gentile onto the tree by the blood of Christ in the first place (Ephesians 2:16–18). "And that He might reconcile them both to God in one body through the cross, thereby putting to death the enmity. And He came and preached peace to you who were afar off and to those who were near. For through Him we both have access by one Spirit to the Father" (Romans 11). She knew they were all engrafted by God.

When God does something, He leaves it up to us to accept it. He's right in raising the bar, but it's never too high. It seems Margaret's parents have been reaching for the bar set before them!

"Here in Ephesians 5:22–33, it tells us of the married life of Spirit-filled believers," read Father.

Mother slightly narrowed her eyes. She knows that passage can easily be taken out of context; however, Father explained it correctly.

"I understand that passage. I will be there for Margaret in every aspect expected of me. I already love her as the church, and I will put myself ahead of her with respect to making safe decisions, as well as to help her with Scripture when she asks me or whatever she needs help with," promised Garth.

"And I want to go to my own husband for what I need. Who better to trust than the one who obeys God?" said Margaret.

"If you both follow every word of God, Mother and I won't need to watch your marriage grow cold," he said.

"And your children will learn by example. That's all we could ever want for them," ended Mother.

"Are you really having kids as in the plural form?" interjected George.

"That's what you have when you're married. Boy, don't you think about anything outside of food?" scolded Harriet

"We would like for you both to join us for lunch after church," said Mother, changing the subject before George starts thinking about his stomach.

"Right, and of course, the church would like to say farewell, including those who won't be attending the wedding on Saturday," predicted Father.

Garth agreed, then stood up to conclude the visit, and reached for his sweater. "Thanks for the Scripture and food. I have something to take care of with my brothers soon as I get home," he said.

"Does it have something to do with us?" questioned Margaret.

"Everything has something to do with us from now on," he said as he waved to the others and walked to the door with her. "I will see you coming down the aisle tomorrow, and I know I'll remember it forever" were his last words to her.

His brothers were outside when he arrived. They were about to decorate their father's car for the wedding once he was home and in the house. He figured he was going to help; however, they didn't want him to see the finished job until morning. The day before, they helped him wax his dark blue 1947 Ford until it mirrored the objects near it, and the needed work that had to be done under the hood was done! His dad was the one who put the needed parts in and swapped out the old tires for new ones. That was their wedding gift from his family. It ran and looked new. He bought it during his last year of high school, which solved a lot of freedom issues, meaning he and

Margaret could spend more time visiting in the biblical study barn. "These animals in here heard enough Scripture to turn them into believers!" Margaret used to say.

That night, Margaret lay on her bed absorbing the silence that encompassed her. She remembered some of the letters they wrote that took each of them on a tour through one another's hearts and minds from across the miles. No letters now. The tour is over. They will pick up where they left off, before he was drafted, by walking down beautiful roads like their favorite ones near home, by holding hands when they want, by looking at each other laughing, and by hearing the other say, "I love you," and to read and pray together. It's her last time to ponder the velvety night sky by herself, to admire the Christmas star in the firmament, and the last to watch the silky sun rising. Soon she'll wake up married, for a lifetime.

The windowsill birds were chirping through the half-opened window. One bounced far enough inside to pick at the clump of hair on Margaret's face, stirring her out of her sleep. Instantly it struck her that the little messengers were telling her it's a special day, by reason of waking her earlier this time. "No wonder they call you feathered friends. Do you also have the antidote for nervous excitement?" she said to their tiny, animated faces.

She flung her blankets on Harriet's bed one last time. One last time Harriet objected. Together they lunged for their dresses, but Harriet still waking up, grabbed at Margaret's. Then Margaret grabbed it back. "Who's the one getting married?" snapped Margaret, in a playful manner.

"Wouldn't that be a nightmare coming in the wrong dress?" roared Harriet.

"Remember that dream you had about how chaotic my wedding was? I once wrote Garth to tell him about it," admitted Margaret.

"What a hilarious dream that was. Everything was mixed up," snickered Harriet. "Hey, when do we leave for the church?"

"With my wedding beginning at 2:00 p.m., we need to be there before one. Mom will probably say eleven fifty-nine though." She laughed. "She calls me, 'the morning bride.' Every day I'll be the morning bride!"

"Never thought I'd say it, but you're a romantic, Margaret. So we have almost three hours to get any loose ends done, and your hair fixed after my chores," affirmed Harriet.

"Right. I need to spend a short time by myself at the church as well, to gather my thoughts. I want to be relatively calm and take every part of this day one step at a time," decided Margaret.

"I agree. I'm going to miss your flying blankets, Big Sis. I'll miss driving with you to Young People's, and the nasty corner is going to miss you too," sighed Harriet.

"I'll miss everything but the corner," said Margaret.

"You missed it before!" Harriet laughed.

"That's funny, I think." Margaret grinned.

"Girls, I need you to help me with my hair and dress. I tried the zipper, but it's too much for me," shouted Mother.

"Be right there," Harriet called back.

Margaret gently picked up her delicate bouquet to set it in its personalized box. Never has she seen such a beautifully designed arrangement in her life. "I shall walk in truth today and always," she spoke out loud.

She packed up her gown with veil, shoes, and personalized box into a life-sized clothing bag. Harriet came back to help her sister with the little details that often have a way of adding up to an extra hour of time.

George and Father were ready to go, although they knew that wasn't about to happen. Mother was still fighting with herself. It wasn't the zipper that continued to make trouble. It was her rebellious hair. Father peeked in the bedroom to see what she was doing and saw her hair in the air with a back comb stuck in it. He backed out to join George at the table. George was eating leftovers like they were his last meal.

"Better not drop any of that on your suit. Mother's hair will stand on end," he joked.

"Isn't that how it always is?" George smiled.

"Your mom looks especially elegant today. I think she's even happy to believe Margaret is thrilled about her future with Garth," supposed Father.

"I'm happy for Margaret. Garth is not the kind of guy to jump in the lake and swim to the other side if things get heated. He'll stay and work it out," said George while grabbing for a cloth to wipe milk from his pants.

"That's a big thing to say." Father agreed.

"I guess I've known that for a long time. I kept in touch through letters too, you know," professed George.

Suddenly three women appeared before them, only Mother in colorful apparel. Somehow her hair turned out for the better, thought Father. Margaret and Harriet wanted to finish preparing in the back room of the church in order to avoid being seen in their gowns.

"We're set to go," announced Mother.

"Let's get this bride to the groom. They've planned long enough," pleaded Harriet.

Margaret peeled back her long dress, which was a fitting outfit prior to the wedding gown, and stepped down into the waiting car. Harriet was already seated inside with her bagged things. Father closed Margaret's door, and George closed Mother's. Today he didn't complain about sitting next to Harriet; she even left her door open for him.

Margaret's heart had much time to speak with God. Every mile was accounted for in terms of prayer and gratitude. As the car climbed the last hill, the formation of the church's peek came into view.

Everyone cleared out of the car to make way for Margaret. Father carried her wedding things inside, and Mother followed next to Harriet who carried her own gown and shoes. George handed Margaret a note, then spun around the other way to search for the right pew to park himself on.

Once inside the back room, Margaret fluffed up her gown, took the precious live bouquet out of the box, then lifted her veil onto her head. Harriet and Mother did the detailing as far as her hair and veil went. Afterward, she lifted her borrowed hooped slip to guide the blue garter in place that Mrs. Roberts gave her. Just then, a knock on the door sounded out, and Margaret's second mother stepped in. "Just to let you know, guests are trickling in. Furthermore, I set the wedding cake out on the dinner table, and the gift table is ready for gifts," reported Mrs. Roberts. "Margaret, you look stunning, and it's only the slip and veil."

"Thank you. The slip didn't come from the store's mannequin, so I had to borrow one. I can't wait to see the cake that your friend designed with you. You have a new skill for when Harriet gets married." Margaret smiled.

"Hey, no wild ideas allowed behind my back." Harriet shuffled, trying to navigate between Shirly and Sharon with Margaret's gown. "You two came just in time to help pour Margaret into her gown, or should I say, pour it over her head and slip. I think it can be done. Just open the back as far as it'll go," conducted Harriet.

When the others left the room for Margaret's time alone, she sat down in a large chair and opened George's note.

It read:

> Margaret, my sister, I love you and will miss you. Sorry for not doing more to make your life better. I'm lazy, but not when it comes to important things such as this note, or the times I took on your chores as a Christmas present to you.
>
> I wrote Garth a few letters because I knew how you felt about him being drafted all those excruciating miles away. I couldn't compete with his supportive words, but I hope this note will be a start. I will write to you even if I'm busier now that I will be doing an extra load of farmwork. I'm proud to be in your wedding party and look forward to seeing you walk up the aisle.
>
> Love, George.

She would later talk with George about his thoughtful note. Next, she read aloud from her Bible.

> Be kindly affectionate to one another with brotherly love, in honor giving preference to one another. (Romans 12:10)

And the two shall become one flesh; so, then they are no longer two, but one flesh. Therefore, what God has joined together, let not man separate. (Mark: 10:8–9)

Two are better than one, because they have a good reward for their labor. For if they fall, one will lift up his companion. But woe to him who is alone when he falls, For he has no one to help him up. Again, if two lie down together, they will keep warm; But how can one be warm alone? Though one may be overpowered by another, two can withstand him. And a three-fold cord is not quickly broken. (Ecclesiastes 4:9–12)

She continued to read 1 Corinthians 13:4–8 and Proverbs 31:10–31.

Right at that time, Garth entered the church with his father and brothers but first looked back at his dad's yellow and black 1955 Mercury. They did a good job decorating it. Ted drove him there; his brother Jerry and Donald, including his father, came in Garth's blue Ford.

He then turned to see a lightly decorated church of white ribbon and bows tied to certain pews. The large wall candles were a magnificent showpiece stationed in the front of the church. He took his place up front with Ted, Donald, and brother-in-law, George. His blue suit matched everything and everyone. He knew Margaret preferred it over the brown one and his uniform.

By this time, the church bloomed with wedding guests that were chatting while waiting. Pastor Dale Linebough was now present, holding his minister's manual. He and Garth exchanged a few words, and the music began with the Pastor's wife, Opal. As she sang the Lord's Prayer, joined by Merriam Hayes on the organ, Margaret and her father moved into view. Her veil descended just below her waist, floating around her hips. An angelic face remained slightly hidden behind it. Her one-of-a-kind gown hung just above the ground—oh, what a longed-for sight! The groom would have to wait until later that day with his private thoughts reserved to say.

The aisle was spread wide with people on each side, both mothers sat upfront, hers on the left and his on the right with his father. Whispers escaped from various pews. Sets of eyes froze into gazes. The older couples remembered back to how it was opposed to younger ones looking ahead to how it might be; time seemed to stand still for both. The maid of honor and bridesmaids went ahead of the father and bride. Their dresses in rainbow colors moved with a light brushing sound.

Margaret's small hands held the bouquet of her…little white Bible. Live white orchids lay swirled on top with lavender ones cascading on long fastened ribbons of white.

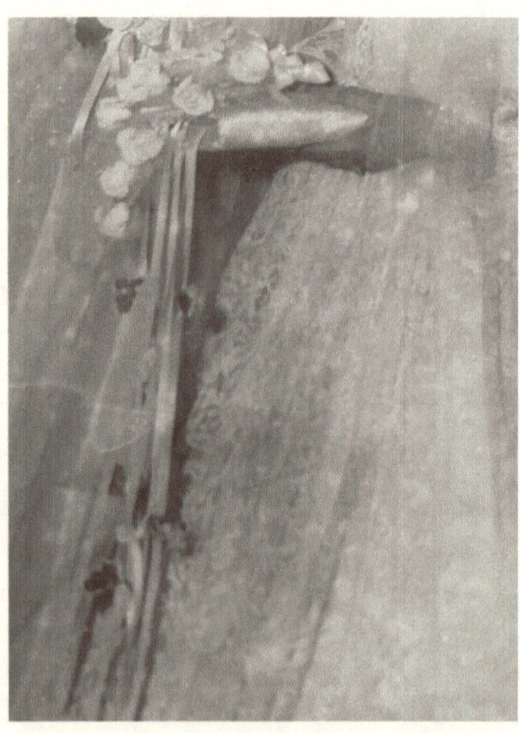

Loved for Life

The Lord took side the morning bride,
her Bible for her bouquet.
A girl who laughed, who loved, and prayed,
was married and carried away.
Her Bible held, did sweetly tell,
of a godly life she'd live,
and the man she met and hoped to get,
God willingly chose to give.
Her gown in white, when touched by light,
glistened with perfect flow,
and fell to her feet adorned in shoes,
that twinkled like pure white snow.
Their vows were said with rings to wed,
her hands in his that day,
foretold their love, their trust and care,
offered together in every way.
Their whole life story, gave God glory,
on every single bend,
and met their King on solid ground,
right unto the very end.

S.S.

Father stood his fair child next to her groom, then stepped aside to watch his oldest daughter become his bride. Mother sat and cried.

With vows now said and rings to wed, they greeted their guests, then turned and stole away for a quiet moment downstairs. Pictures followed while guests were seated, with dinner about to begin.

"Two more pictures. I need the parents with the bride and groom," announced the professional photographer. The pro was Margaret's cousin, Howard. This wedding was kept in the family for the most part and was every bit as lovely as they had hoped. Not a lot of decoration filled Birchardville Baptist Church; nevertheless, Garth told Margaret that she was all the beauty the church needed.

Dinner was splendid, and the young people sang while they cut their cake, singing, "Love and marriage go together like a horse and carriage, you can't have one without the other." The gifts were grand. Much of what they needed was now provided for their apartment in Jacksonville, Alabama, where they would be staying near the military's base; however, she did not yet know that he rented it. And that wasn't how the day ended. The whole wedding party drove through Garth's hometown of Montrose, then to the village of Rush where Margaret graduated. The streamers on the back of the 1955 Merc rushed wildly from side to side, each one curling around the one next to it, then breaking free only to do it all over again. A few red and white flowers disappeared from the car after fluttering for some of the trip, by completely reversing when they picked up speed until they just couldn't hold on any longer. Their "just married" sign stayed safe in the back window. It included the words, "Each for the other, both for the Lord."

The last stop was Margaret's parents' house sixty-five miles away for dinner. Her mother put on an exceptional dinner for someone who couldn't fully dress herself earlier that day; God was in everything. Father prayed over the food. Both Margaret's and Garth's family, including a few friends, enjoyed a dinner and day to never be forgotten.

It's nine o'clock, time for the newlyweds to leave for the motel in Green Gables, New Milford Pennsylvania, twenty miles from his parents' home, then back again for church in the morning.

"I can't believe how perfect this day went. So many times, I called myself Mrs. Roberts over the last several months," said Margaret.

"And I called us Mr. and Mrs. Roberts ever since Valentine's Day when the mailman trucked up your rippled driveway with a 'special delivery!' His old car had permanent rattles from every driveway he chugged up and down." Garth chuckled.

"And Mrs. Condon knew it was something special because the mailman only goes right up to houses if he has parcels to deliver," related Margaret.

As they laughed themselves around the last corner, the town's lights were suddenly upon them. The young married couple looked on with anticipation. People in their vehicles stopped to watch them drive by. The chaotic streamers laid calm whenever they stopped, then viciously ripped through the air again, gaining attention from passersby.

"This looks like the motel. I didn't realize it would look so quaint. I like it," Margaret said, observing the old-fashioned wagon wheel and burning coal oil lamp under the motel's lit-up canopy.

The man at the desk raised his head, then his eyebrows, studying the dressy couple that stood before him. "Name please," he asked.

"Mr. and Mrs. Roberts," verified Garth.

"Here's your key. Don't mess the place. Don't wreck the place, and don't leave the place without dropping the key off," he declared.

"Uh okay. Thank you. You have a nice place. Wouldn't think of wrecking it." Margaret smiled.

Hand in hand they walked into their quaint little room. Much time was offered in prayer to their Lord, for it was Him that brought them together.

Morning dawned; and Margaret was already up with a small prepared breakfast of bread, butter, and boiled eggs from mother's kitchen back home. After church service, they would spend the afternoon with her parents and the evening with his. Tuesday, they left for Alabama for military duty and the secret apartment.

CHAPTER 9

Apartment for 3, Gunshots,
and the Delivery Room

The five days of honeymooning down Blue Ridge Parkway was a beautiful drive. Being spring, wildflowers stretched for miles, never running out. Every now and then, deer would flood the roadway in pursuit of fields for new grass. They'd leave their fawns in hiding while they gathered to feast. Occasionally wild turkeys peered out of the ditch but were inclined to stay put for fear of being struck by what must have looked like aliens with bulging eyes whizzing past them.

"Where are we staying when we arrive? You mentioned before about a place with other people that we'd have to share a bathroom with. I suppose I can get used to that," assumed Margaret.

"Nope, we won't be staying that close to anyone or be sharing a bathroom. I was trying to keep it a secret, but I guess I can't anymore. It's the kind of apartment you wanted, private and cozy," he promised.

"Oh, I can't wait to see it! Our own place? It's better than I thought. And I can't wait to meet the chaplain and his wife. I think a handful of our letters consisted of them mixed in with our own news," she warmly said. I want to thank them for all their spiritual help when you struggled with opposition from some of the Army guys; not many Christians to talk with, you said. I imagine it was

"

more difficult than your letters expressed," she acknowledged, with a comforting hand in reach for his.

"Yeah, and if it wasn't for them and your letters, I might have died of a wound worse than in combat, loneliness," he specified.

"Well, the loneliness is over. Like I basically said in one of my letters, 'Pretty soon you'll be trying to figure out how to live with me,'" warned Margaret with a loving smile.

"That I can figure out, them I can't. Nothing is as bad as living with other men and their memories of wives or girlfriends when its late at night. I know as much about their problems than any psychiatrist. And I have a better answer than they would give, 'Gotta get Jesus!'" he testified. "Look, we're coming into Jacksonville, Alabama. This drive was worth every mile this time, just knowing we're here together," said Garth.

They parked and sat before their apartment located on the edge of the village, locking eyes in excitement of their first place. Exhausted from the extensive trip, they climbed out of the car to first look at the inside, then bring their belongings in. The walls were a welcoming soft yellow. The bedroom was elongated, and Margaret thought it to be peculiar. The whole place measured twenty by thirty.

"I like it. I'll be happy here in Alabama's little yellow apartment. There's room for a crib in this bedroom. I'm impressed that the entire place comes furnished too. I'll add our things and get this place in order. I'll whip it into shape," explained Margaret.

"No doubt you will. However, you won't have to whip me into shape for as long as I'm on the Army base. They keep me shaped up, but I can't wait till they ship me out of there altogether. Right now, I'm just looking forward to coming home to you and your cooking every day," he added.

"I'll be doing my best," she said. "Let's get our things from the car so I can start with our bedroom. Night isn't far away at this point. We can work on the kitchen in the morning," bargained Margaret.

That night, they settled on the couch in front of the jumbo picture window, relieved to be home. The bedroom was arranged and the mattress sheeted in. As Garth sat and listened, Margaret made an interesting point.

"Though we were over 1,200 miles apart, we used to gaze at the same stars and moon through our own section of sky. Just think how it sort of connected our physical eyes while God connected our hearts," noted Margaret.

"From now on, we'll be only five miles apart when I'm on the base in Ft. McCullen. We'll be watching the stars nightly from this window," he said, closing for the night.

Mornings in Jacksonville are generally pleasant due to the quiet village. The only alarm clock is their own by reason of no loud traffic or horns to wake them. It's an ideal location for a young couple; after all, planning to have a family includes strategy in more ways than one.

That morning, Margaret began organizing each room after breakfast starting with the living room. Garth moved the furniture several times before she decided that the way it was was the best way. He was glad the washroom was unchangeable! In addition, they added their wedding gifts of appliances, towels for different jobs, a set of pots and pans, framed pictures, and a couple throw rugs. "There's nothing like words of welcome on a mat at the door," insisted Margaret.

"True, considering the chaplain and his wife, Peggy, will want to visit us soon. Tomorrow I'm due back to the base, and surely, they'll be anxious to meet you and to see our place," he added.

Margaret settled into Jacksonville extremely quick. The Army chapel became their church home, and they were fully on board in ministry there. She became a friend to everyone involved, and Peggy was genuinely motherlike toward her.

In June, Margaret learned she was pregnant. The doctor on the Army post confirmed it. When Garth came home at 6:00 p.m., he barreled through the door to make the usual statement of being home and ready to eat. Margaret was sitting at the unset table. It was evident that no supper had been prepared.

"Why are you in your nightgown, hon?" he asked.

"I haven't felt well some of the day. I saw the town doctor today though, and he said, 'don't know what it is, but it's going to take months to resolve.'" Margaret smiled.

"He doesn't know?" echoed Garth.

"Right, he doesn't know if it'll be a boy or girl! We'll be needing a rocking chair!" announced Margaret.

With the front door still open, they cried with excitement, not caring who or what might be strolling by and stopping to slip in a foot and a look inside. God received praise through gratitude and prayer. Both families were notified thanks to Grandmother Roberts, as in the past, for having a phone.

Peggy vowed to take care of Margaret. Plus, she rounded up other Army wives with plans going into place to help when the baby arrives. News like this explodes like a bomb shell after it drops from the doctor's mouth. People are speedier in reaching others than any newspaper, letter, or plane; and the best part is that it's good news. In those days, parents and young couples lived in uncertainty of the news because it could mean talk of war.

They lived each day with and for the Lord. Time for devotions was, as usual, critical to begin the day and end it. Margaret had never been so thrilled—her own place, her own husband, her own ministry and her own baby on the way. Just one thing was missing, one thing that would become a part of their family for a lifetime and would be well used, the universal family rocking chair of significance.

Saturday, to-town day, is the day to shop for food and possibly a few baby items. Margaret dressed in record time, trying to fit herself in a dress that seems to have its side seams snugger than usual.

"It's to-town day, Garth, and I'd like to go shopping, considering I'm feeling up to it. This morning sickness is lessening in severity, giving me more opportunity to get outdoor things accomplished. The doctor on the Army base compiled a list of things he wants me to do daily, and walking is one of them," explained Margaret. "Let's just calculate what we can spend in accordance with your pay before we leave."

"We should have an extra twenty-five dollars as a result of the car burning less fuel on the trip here than I figured. I've been saving it for a rainy day. I think you need a few things to wear and a comfortable chair," he suggested.

"That's just what I need," she decided.

After parking and walking up to the secondhand store's bay window, there it was, a unique rocking chair! "Oh, look, Garth, every time I need something, I find it. It's just like when my parents bought my graduation outfit or when I saw my wedding dress. How can God go from controlling all those Old Testament wars to today's complicated wars and still think about the small things that we need?"

"He's provider of all things small and large. Can't limit Him to certain things only. A need is a need, and we're in need," he preached.

Upon entering the store, someone else was looking at the chair. Margaret's heart hurt for a split second since that was the only rocking chair for miles. However, the moment that person strolled far enough from it, Garth scooped it up and headed for the clerk behind the counter. He paid him the twelve dollars according to the hanging price tag, and Margaret opened the exit door for her husband and her chair.

Things were coming together for them on behalf of friends lending their items to use, such as a high chair and crib. The baby clothes were for keeping. But as the months passed, no one knew of the great danger ahead until Margaret was brought into the delivery room. God took over that day, for there would not have been a wife and baby to bring home.

Gunshots rang out drowning Margaret's sporadic cries of unimaginable discomfort followed by the blasting guns in sequence. This was not a great place for a shooting range, or maybe not a great place for a hospital; nevertheless, the doctor and nurses on the base worked together with precision, missing no detail from their prior years of training, though it was rare that they had to complete the turn of a baby laying crosswise in the womb. Under the circumstances, Chaplain Harris immediately left to inform Garth that his wife and baby may not survive according to the doctor's level of concern. The news sent him looking to Jesus through the gunpowdered sky in the bitter cold, saying, "Lord, a need is a need, and we're in need. I ask You, oh great physician, to give our baby and Margaret a life to live for You. Guide the doctor with instructions and move his hands as your own, if it be your will. Amen."

Margaret, being so far from home, couldn't think of where she was or of anything except the very moment beginning after the last, with each one the same. Her breath stayed in her lungs until they threatened to either burst or rebreathe the dusty air. Suddenly she recaptured a memory of when she and Garth stood in the sun's rays with millions of circulating particles; they were warmed, and she was beautiful. The natural exaggeration of the silhouette trees and rays pouring through them have led some writers into an unreturnable reality while writing. Margaret believed these natural abilities to be a safe mystery to explore when one is given over to God in that the mind is as deep as God makes it. But no one told her in all her twenty years that this amount of pain was possible, with no comparison.

It took two hours in getting Garth to the base to find out what all happened. Is the baby a son or daughter, or more importantly, a live son or daughter? Would his wife be waiting for him with her life or without it? What did God decide?

"Mr. Roberts," said a familiar voice. "Over here by the window."

He looked over to see the doctor admiring a sleeping child through an inside window. It was there to keep air and others from mixing with premature babies.

"Is this my…," his voice trailed off.

"This is your miracle daughter," replied the doctor.

"What about my…," his words failing him.

"Your wife is in recovery. Both were through a difficult time. The baby was crosswise in the womb, and Margaret kept passing out, worrying us each time for fear of her slipping away. You can't always tell with this type of delivery based on the lack of medical inventions to alert us of any changes in status. However, that's why we have training and gut reactions. Therefore, it's called a practice. I like to think of it as practicing under the Physician over all physicians," he explained.

"Well, God will guide for lack or not of equipment. You partnered with Him today, and I thank you for putting Him before your task," said Garth, stressing the point that this truly is the reason they survived.

A four-pound, ten-ounce January baby, Elizabeth Lynn (Beth) was kept in the hospital for four weeks. Margaret was able to leave after five days, although she felt it wasn't easy to pack up and go without Beth. She had their bedroom ready for this day for months. When she did come home, the joy of parenting took over with belated kisses, modeling homemade baby gowns and demonstrations of sponge baths for Dad followed by diaper pinning.

Their engagement from one year ago this February fourteenth brought back wonderful memories of being at home for Margaret, such as when the mail man disappeared from the kitchen window, then popped up with a package that he dropped on the doorstep. She ripped, then cut at that parcel until glints of light caught the diamond in her ring, seizing her expression with its array of reflected colors.

Their families back home were excited, especially Margaret's family since they had no grandchildren or a niece until now. George liked the new addition of uncle in front of his name whenever Margaret addressed his letters as "Dear Uncle George." Aunt Harriet felt doubled in age due to how old it sounded, but there was no alternative. So she accepted it. Mr. and Mrs. Roberts were grandparents two years prior to Elizabeth; nonetheless, they were thrilled. The advice of Margaret's "second mom" was welcomed on a few accounts. By February twentieth, they were back in church at the Army chapel. They showed up with Beth in a basket that they called an ark and had her dedicated to the Lord.

May brought a double surprise visit. Both sets of parents came to see the three of them, and the second surprise was the fact that they came together! Garth and Margaret were grateful that they truly considered each other as family in the full sense. It was a perfect time to visit now that Beth had crept up in weight and was beginning to sit upright though she was still wobbly. The entire family visit left everyone with a lasting impression and a lasting amazement in God. It reinforced Margaret's desire to dedicate everything to God in prayer that life puts on her, whether good or not.

By June, Peggy Harris and Margaret began teaching VBS (Vacation Bible School) in the little country churches. Naturally Beth went along in her ark. Margaret used her experience from her Sunday school classes she taught back home. Opal's mentoring increased not only her ability but her confidence in what the Lord desired for those whom she directed to His Word. She vowed to look at everything from the standpoint of the mind of Christ and continued to form responsible intelligence as not only a natural woman but as a spiritual woman; the Bible does not only teach the way of salvation but the way of spiritual sanity.

> I Beseech you therefore, brethren, by the mercies of God, that you present your bodies a living sacrifice, holy, acceptable to God, which is your reasonable service. And do not be conformed to this world, but be transformed by the renewing of your mind, that you may prove what is that good and acceptable and perfect will of God. (Romans 12:1–2)

For "who has known the mind of the Lord that he may instruct Him?" But we have the mind of Christ. (1 Corinthians 2:16)

The feel of the pre-summery breeze increased in warmth each day. The sun lifted new seedlings, strengthening their infant stems and boosted baby tree trunks from beneath the frost-free ground. Soon they would be towers for insects to climb on, live in, eat from, and hide under. The sun took charge over the ground with grass of green velvet, along with the birth of leaves from waiting buds on trees. Garth and Margaret, as anyone else, looked forward to days like these. It's baby Beth's first summer to discover what God does in the outdoors. Nothing will be understood, of course, but learning what grass feels like while on walks with Mom and Dad is a good place to begin.

CHAPTER 10

Bible College, 3 Girls and 1 Boy

Hallelujah! It's July fifth, still 1957, and Garth has been discharged from the Army! Of course, this meant that a wife is also released for the reason of her life paralleling certain aspects of his Army life; they faced the fear of a war together that could have torn apart family life for who knows how long.

Their freedom brought with it a plan to enroll in Bible college. For some, this is where the tender soul sits on a balancing scale of hearing God's call and obeying Him to such an idea. As exciting as it may be though, it would all be pointless if one could not identify with His deity. Garth and Margaret had an open, willing mind and humble heart toward God; and in prayer for the short duration in receiving their answer, the answer was yes! Arrangements were made, and they jetted off to stay at Camp El Rancho Depaz in Owego, New York, with both attending practical Bible training school at the college. The camp put them to work as counselors. Margaret did some cooking, and Garth took care of the horses and trail rides as extras. The Lord was well represented in their character and teaching material; however, after one year there, they needed to move into an apartment with their growing family.

Between 1957–1960, two more daughters were born, Voris Marie in 1959 at the hospital in Garth's hometown (Montrose, Pennsylvania) and Esther Jean in 1960 in the same place Margaret went to nursing school (Johnson City, New York). Both places were located near Owego New York.

Margaret put countless miles on her chair with their three little girls. Really, it was a twenty-four-hour, all-season rocking chair. Many nights you would see a shadow on the wall of a little head finally dip onto her chest fast asleep. On outings, people would lower their eyes to see the two content babies floating by in their "wicker arks," just staring into the sky until a strange face appeared and hung in their sight for a moment. But considering the size of Voris, the leaden basket was soon replaced with a carriage.

One Saturday afternoon, after the girls were carried to bed and tucked in for a nap, they sat at the kitchen window. The sun was spilling inside the apartment, lighting up the entire kitchen and floor. Margaret got up to walk on the sunshine thinking about the superiority God gave it in order to sustain all life. Later that evening, the sunset was extraordinary in the sense that it looked large enough and close enough to the earth to step onto. Nothing could filter such power from its eerie but lovely glow. The whole day was spent doing homework and taking turns attending to the kids.

College had been going well since commencing in 1957 to the conclusion date in sight. "We have completed enough homework for the rest of the week," cheered Margaret.

"Ah yes. These past three years took me up and down my Bible. I've been through it more times than that stop sign on our corner. I must say, we've learned a load about spiritual and emotional intelligence in this challenging program. Three years of college and a lifetime of ministry ahead," he half whispered, as to not stir the girls awake.

As the sun's face went from a blushing shade to seriously reddening, their furniture and clothes took on different hues while Margaret commented on the Lord's ways, "I came to a better understanding that my ways and thoughts are not the same as God's (Isaiah 55:8–9). The Bible is only part of His mind mixed with much of His character. And our redemption will remove us from living under Adam and Eve's failure, back into the garden of life with God."

Garth was about to comment and give Scripture when they heard a thud. A bird had crash-landed against the window and dropped to the ground, ruffling its feathers to regain its ability to lift itself to safety, but it was Margaret who opened the window to bring him into safety. She figured she better examine the dizzy bird. It reminded her of the windowsill birds back home that had a great amount of trust, pecking her hair some mornings that laid piled on her cheek.

"True. When we're with God, we'll have the personalized experience of a one-on-one conversation with Him and have a full understanding," he finished saying once he saw the bird get its second wind. Still thinking of the unharmed bird, he pointed out an interesting truth that he had been meaning to tell Margaret, and it applied to what she said. "Though the tree of life was offered in the garden of Eden after the creation of man, then was denied because of the fall of man (Genesis 2:17), it will again be offered at the final redemption at the Lord's throne (Revelation 22:2). And we will live without failure this time."

Graduation day was upon Garth and Margaret. Once again, they're having a double grad! He received his pastoral diploma, and she completed her Bible diploma, including a counseling and pastor's wife course, the main course being Christian education. She was also certified in ETTA (Educational Teachers Training Association) from Moody Bible Institute.

They ended up moving back home to the Montrose area, where Garth is from, to live. From there, they drove every week to their home church of Birchardville Baptist to do the youth ministry with the teenaged group. They're back where they met and doing the same ministry they attended! Garth had the privilege of gladly accepting pastoral work on top of it all. With an additional privilege, he and Margaret agreed to do visitation outside the church. During this time, he worked three jobs, as a transport driver, a log and lumber worker, and farm work.

Soon after, both were commissioned as missionary assistants to Native American ministry. They served under Faith Baptist Indian Mission and began their deputation ministry in raising support for their up and coming move to Six Nations Reservation for ministry near Brantford, Ontario, in Canada with the Seneca aboriginal people. All Six Nations are represented at Brantford. The Seneca also have their own reservations in New York state.

Meanwhile, Garth became a deacon around the same time their son, Arthur Herman, was born. It was a marvelous moment in their lives when he emerged into the world. They'd stand over him as he slept, thanking God for another healthy baby and that their fourth miracle was a boy! Margaret just knew the baby was going to be a boy after she and the Lord spoke through Scripture. She rocked him every day with songs of praise to the Lord. All her children came to know the meaning of that single most important piece of furniture as their mom's spiritual chair.

Margaret's family was extremely pleased to have her and her family living so close. Mr. And Mrs. Roberts were thrilled that they were living in their hometown. It wasn't often that they could take the grandkids to see each set of grandparents since three jobs and three days a week of church business was continual. It was especially surprising though when it happened to work out that the whole bunch could be together at once. As far as the teenaged ministry went, Margaret established solid studies on Christ. One was particularly comprehensive, compelling the students to study their mind and heart toward God. She used Scriptures (1 Corinthians 6:19–20) to explain "we are not our own, but belong to God," and to "love Him with all their heart, soul, and strength" (Deuteronomy 6:5). She found creative explanations alongside Scripture in providing them with truth, giving them much afterthought on the matter. She told them if they don't take the walls down in their mind that block God and His word, how then can He renew it every day (Romans 12:2)? She went on to say that the walls are usually there by reason of sin in their life. "When you honestly examine yourselves, and expose your sin to Jesus in repentance, He will free you indeed" was her conclusion (John 8:31–36). And "it sounds intense, but where we end in life, is where we begin our eternity, so you want to end well," she'd add.

Preaching Jesus was number one to her, and leaving lasting impressions in one's mind and heart was important, which she attested to. She believed the Holy Spirit was the one that took what the students were taught and cultivated it in them. They learned that they had a loving Creator, sin breaker, peacemaker, and forgiving Savior to turn to with their sins and prayer requests. Margaret adhered her soul and spirit to Christ, making each day a building block of fundamental truths. Her husband, children, and ministry were covered in prayer, leaving virtually no room for evil to get a foothold in her ability to love and teach.

While Margaret was engaged in reading her Bible one afternoon, a feeling of urgency came over her. With her head bowed, she asked the Lord to look after Garth. He was down a narrow backroad that led him to a mountaintop with his transport truck. The boss's son, Bill, who decided to go with him that trip convinced Garth to take the shortcut to wheel their load of ash logs to the Spalding Bat Factory in Troy Pennsylvania. Those logs were going to be turned into baseball bats! But Garth wasn't sure if they'd make it there when he saw what they were in for.

Getting up the highest hill was treacherous enough. Now they had to go down. The faces of his family entered his crowded mind, which was filling with fear of possibly losing the load. It was a grip-tight slow roll into the abyss that would either leave them remarkably intact or mangled.

Twenty gears, a five and a four, billowing smoke poured from the screaming brake shoes before they could get near halfway down. Crushing thoughts pushed in hard and had to be pushed back out; otherwise, any hope would be abolished. The charred smell was clearly from heated metal, crumbling like cheese. The whole truck quaked as though it was about to explode. A narrow, maximum two-ton bridge over the Loyalsock River looked up at them with their fifty-year-old boards; surely, they would threaten to buckle thought Garth. With no brakes left but the emergency brake, the truck nailed that bridge, almost bursting those boards apart like popsicle sticks. The weather-beaten boards on the ends of the sides did come apart and shot upright, taking off in flight way ahead of the truck's nose.

They landed in the river's whirlpools that immediately sucked them in, taking them downstream, never to be seen again.

Margaret had no idea of the incident taking place. All she knew was that she felt there was a need for prayer. The girls were napping while she rocked Arthur. Supper was brewing up a fantastic aroma throughout the apartment of chicken soup and homemade bread while she spoke to the Lord.

Garth was crawling the wounded rig back to town by emergency brake only, then had a servicing done on it. The brakes were decrepit. They broke down into chunks of metal, and the brake lines were dangling, stretched past their capability.

Garth staved off his hunger until he got home. He had a meal worth waiting for, and she got a backwoods story worth hearing. He told her how the big rig collided with the bridge, buckling the weary boards that had fifty years of seasons beat down on them, then how it crushed what little life remained in them.

"Well, good luck, or should I say good idea to pray on those back roads. I'll be in the prayer chair every day I suppose, if you're going to take chances like that," she voiced in a cute way as if to be releasing the stressful images in her mind. Garth smiled to himself because when Margaret gets upset, she can be comical.

The bridge's capacity for weight hit an all-time high that day, delivering a rare experience to remember! (Two years later the bridge was repaired by those who sat in a group each day at lunchtime, discussing possibilities on what happened to cave its structure. Garth informed certain people afterward about the incident, but funny enough, it appeared the bridge workers were in the dark.)

"Have the girls eaten enough today?" asked Garth, knowing payday is still a few days away.

"Yes, you were so late in getting home that I fed them and then again before bed. This time, they explored the soup under the floating crackers. Usually, they just eat the crackers and push the soup aside," she answered, still thinking about the pressure he was under and that God had her praying.

"How was Arthur today?" he inquired.

"He had a good day. Beth played with him off and on, keeping him amused for me while I was cooking. Those two have figured out that if one laughs, the other follows until their voices merge into one." Margaret chuckled.

"Would have liked to have witnessed that. Just to see the look on their faces," he wished.

"Yes, but I must tell you the greatest part of the day. It happened in my rocking chair. As you remember, we prayed for the kids before they were born, and today Beth came to me wanting to accept Jesus. I took her little five-year-old mind and heart to a place in the Bible where she could understand how this is possible for her" (John 1:12). But as many as received Him, to them, He gave the right to become children of God to those who believe in His name. 'I write to you, little children, because your sins are forgiven you for His name's sake' (1John 2:12). Then we sang, 'Jesus Loves Me,'" she exclaimed, nearly waking Arthur.

"That's the best news ever, five years old and beginning her way through salvation. What a cherished moment for you. A lot is taking place in that chair. I would have really liked to have witnessed that too," he said, then added, "No matter the age, it has nothing to do with the state of the child. It's His name's sake why we're saved." They marveled at the thought of their daughter's new relationship with Jesus.

"This is what Christ was martyred for, this and the souls ahead of us in our ministries," declared Margaret. "For You were slain, And have redeemed us to God by Your blood Out of every tribe and tongue and people and nation" (Revelation 5:9).

They spent the rest of the evening curled up on the couch together, staring through their heritage of the magnificent dark velvet sky saturated with stars (Deuteronomy 4:19).

They're unquestionably positioned by the hand of God, allowed at times by Him to suddenly detach from their position, racing through space and time, trailing a tail of tinsel.

CHAPTER 11

Ministry Upon Ministry, the Early Years

It's 1963, and many churches took up the challenge to support Garth and Margaret. Six Nations Reserve gained two solid Christian immigrants to their Canadian reservation, plus their four kids the ages of six, four, three, and one. They were given a house at Garlow Line to live in, which was much appreciated.

Margaret being nonaboriginal was something for the aboriginal people to consider and reconsider. Their delay in decision-making was perfectly acceptable considering the lives some of them and their family members lived; trust is earned, not thrown into the wind.

Their ministry began with missionaries Robert and Edna Johnson at Garlow Line Baptist Church, primarily in outreach, youth ministries, and Sunday school. God was in it from the beginning! Included was Bethany Baptist church, "And He led them out as far as Bethany, and He lifted up His hands and blessed them" (Luke 24:50).

Both churches are under the fellowship of Indian Baptist churches. There they had prayer meetings the same night as Bible Seekers Club with forty kids and thirty from Garlow Line Baptist Church. Margaret was the lead teacher of the adult ladies Bible study and the Bible club for teen girls. She had a staff of women and men to teach who then helped with the ongoing ministries.

Sunday school averaged forty adults and sixty-five teens and children at Bethany Baptist. At Garlow Line Baptist, they had twenty-five adults and forty-five teens and children. The a.m. service was at Bethany with the p.m. service at Garlow Line, then a combined evening service. Sometimes they forgot to breathe between it all. (Much later, Garth would begin a Bible school in 1976 that he would teach all over the USA and Canadian reservations.)

Garth and Margaret had a lovely trail mix of youth before them. The reason of the mix was a few nonaboriginal youths in the same ministry, interacting with all the kids, including their own kids being part aboriginal, though they were younger. It wasn't like the wildflowers that weren't growing up together back when Margaret was eleven (chapter 1). She loved how creative the Lord was while admiring the girls and boys with long flowing hair of deepest midnight and eyes to match! And it's funny how people prepare to buy and lather themselves with oily products to achieve a smooth artificial suntan only to have it fade during the months of winter. *It takes work to match our sisters and brothers!* she thought.

Margaret believed everyone to be equal and in the image of God yet stuffed with different gifts and talents, but she wasn't sure when she might see these things. "Our first week and barely a word from the youth," she said to Garth.

"I think we'll have to give them time to decide whether or not we can be trusted. Some children come from a hard background," he cautioned.

"Right. I haven't forgotten. I'm for them, and if it takes a week longer, that's perfectly fine. I believe so many of our youth have had their spirit broken by the demands and expectations of the world," she acknowledged. "The spirit of a man will sustain him in sickness, But who can bear a broken spirit" (Proverbs 18:14). "A wholesome tongue is a tree of life, But perverseness in it breaks the spirit" (Proverbs 15:4). And, "A merry heart makes a cheerful countenance, But by sorrow of the heart the spirit is broken" (Proverbs 15:13).

"Don't be discouraged, but it may take another six months," he forewarned.

"Six months! Well, I suppose we aren't going anywhere any time soon, so I have all the time it takes. The Lord answers prayer and will perfect that which concerns me (Psalm 138:8)," she said, with thoughtfulness.

"It's something like not being able to rush your pregnancies." He smiled, ending the conversation to attend to Arthur and the girls.

Suddenly, a fleet of teens stormed past their place, charging ahead of one another as if they were being chased. Margaret looked out to find the answer; they were having a race on the warm end-of-September day. It had been a chilly month for most of the days, but today was mild—loads of dry leaves, some with freckles, rained down, spreading over the unseen ground in an array of colors. The kids loved to race through them, then gather thousands into a mound as high and large as possible.

Afterward they'd pick up the smaller children, with one turn at a time, and toss him or her into the tall blanket of colors. Sometimes they'd have to go looking for the missing child who purposely stayed hidden under the blended smells of nature. As the evening sunset faithfully approached, Margaret watched their tall, fleeting shadows running alongside them for home. She was warmed by the playful scene she watched out her window, now thinking of how their shadowed bodies were between the ground's surface and the light.

Not long after, winter came with little warning, and it came early! Snow was cast over the wet, freckled leaves, at least the ones that didn't end up in the nearby rivers and lakes. Soon the bottom boughs of Christmas trees touched the snow. Some were buried for small animals to use as a haven. Nevertheless, there were outdoor activities on the reservation for everyone such as survival skill training in fishing, hunting, rock-flint fires, trapping, shelter building, snowshoeing, and navigation in wooded areas. The teenagers displayed their ideas on how to survive both weather and hunger as a project.

A lot of fun and serious Christian learning happens on these reservations, but so is there a lot of spiritual teardowns from outsiders who disagreed with the Lord Jesus heading up the programs and churches. However, Garth and Margaret handled that with Scripture and prayer. God's love and their love for God and His children gave them perseverance, and His protection was ever present.

Therefore take up the whole armor of God,
that you may be able to withstand in the evil day,

and having done all, to stand. Stand therefore, having girded your waist with truth, having put on the breastplate of righteousness, and having shod your feet with the preparation of the gospel of peace; above all, taking the shield of faith with which, you will be able to quench all the fiery darts of the wicked one. And take the helmet of salvation, and the sword of the Spirit, which is the word of God, praying always with all prayer and supplication in the Spirit, being watchful to this end with all perseverance and supplication for all the saints. (Ephesians 6:13–18)

Yet in all these things we are more than conquerors through Him who loved us. (Romans 8:37)

Prayer is effective only when there is completeness in Christ—take up the whole armer of God (Oswald Chambers, *My Utmost for His Highest*, Dec. 16).

But let all those who rejoice put their trust in You; Let them ever shout for joy, because You defended them; Let those who also love Your name be joyful in You. For You, oh Lord, will bless the righteous; With favor You will surround him as with a shield. (Psalm 5:11–12)

One night, Margaret looked at the many things her rocking chair stood for. It was her personal devotions chair, a Bible story time chair, a hymnal, and prayer chair, plus the chair of emotional comfort for the children. Garth said it was her daily altar. Later, it would become her memorial to all who knew her.

Some months later, in June 1964, they added Camp Owendi (Seneca, meaning ready to harvest), to their ministry located at

Collins Centre, New York, right off the Cattaraugus Reservation. (Faith Baptist Indian Missions which is also a part of Six Nations.)

Margaret was a natural teacher and leader, a wonderful pastor's wife and mother. She did fit in on the reservation, as well as at the camp once it became clear to every heart that she was there for them and not herself. Camp Owendi was located about two and a half hours from where they lived in Brantford, Ontario. They had an average of eighty campers per week with twelve staff volunteers. Margaret oversaw the cooking and domestics. They built these ministries up in number. Among the many ongoing positions, Margaret drove the school bus van" to and from camp which seated sixteen passengers. Bouncing down the dusty roads with singing kids through the miles was a common picture. Even the ladies were bussed to their musicals and conferences.

The camp was on a hill with an empty field that Margaret could see over when checking on her three girls playing in the tiny creek. Since they were too young for the teen camp, Margaret let them explore the creek and the old barn which was used as a chapel.

The leading of the Lord continued down the many roads and trails and paths of ministry, all teaching one way to Christ. A lot of kids were saved in those times of effective ministering, as well as some adults.

During this time of 1964–1965, children were brought to their home for the time it took Children's Aid to find a place for them to stay. Margaret was a mother around the clock, in conjunction with teaching. Her rocking chair served several children besides her own. The small children who had no sanctuary found one in the arms of that rocking chair with Margaret when they came to stay.

Next to this ministry, they were invited to have house meetings on the west end of the Six Nations Reserve, which soon expanded to the point that it became apparent they needed to meet in something larger. That's when a building was purchased, renovated, and became Faith Baptist Chapel. This is how reservation life was for the next few years though it would take a book to reveal more of the incredible journey.

In 1967, their last baby, Rebecca (Becky), was born. She arrived five years after Arthur. She looked like a porcelain doll in her tiny sleeping gowns and could be mistaken for one if she didn't move. Mom and Dad were thrilled once again with another healthy baby girl. She would be protected to no end by her family now that her siblings were old enough to help watch over her. As all their children, she too was dedicated to the Lord.

Margaret had her life filled to the brim, for at this time, they took on the addition of the leadership role of Bethany Mission, which joined with Faith Baptist Chapel. Everything she did was a ministry, but there were days when she needed to take time out to breathe and expand on family time, especially with a new baby. She had to be guarded from overdoing it due to becoming overwhelmed in such deep involvement of caring for a multitude.

One morning in prayer, Garth asked the Lord for Scripture in helping Margaret. He was directed to Philemon 1:6, "That the sharing of your faith may become effective by the acknowledgment of every good thing which is in you in Christ Jesus," leaving him to ask, "Where, Lord?" And it came to him quickly: (1) to your wife, she's your first ministry; (2) to your children; (3) to your church; (4) to your community where you live. This has been his motto in life and ministry ever since.

By the time Rebecca was one year old, Garth and Margaret were pastoring the two churches with Bethany Baptist Church as the official crisis home to manage. She took in pregnant girls, some only the age of fourteen. They learned biblical tools needed to mother their children with. She taught them to cook plus basic, then moderate first-aid training. The youngest of girls waited for Children's Aid to find homes for them with their babies. Many of the girls were saved before they left. Older girls left to be on their own once they were able to, but no one left without knowing who Jesus was.

The Lord led Margaret into what seemed like an ever-spiraling world of problems and suffering; however, more importantly, He led her and them through it. "Those who wait on the Lord shall walk and not faint" (Isaiah 40:31). "The righteous cry out, and the Lord hears, and delivers them out of all their troubles" (Psalm 34:17). Plus, "But the salvation of the righteous is from the Lord; He is their strength in the time of trouble. And the Lord shall help them and deliver them; He shall deliver them from the wicked, and save them, because they trust in Him" (37:39–40).

In it all, her own children continued to find fun in searching for activities to do outdoors with the others. Some of the fun they were seeking back then would be frowned upon today with no real good reason.

One winter day, when the four Roberts siblings ventured out from the parsonage next to Garlow Line Baptist Church where they were living, they noticed several "somethings" skimming alongside the frozen bulrushes at the end of the field. They stood in wonder of the unfamiliar sight. Arthur was young but brave. He stepped out to unravel the mystery, but his sisters pulled him behind themselves to go first. They followed in a single file through the snow drifts on a narrow-packed trail leading to the bulrushes. It stretched across the field, then snaked into the bush. Arthur was trying to pass, but the snow was too deep to veer off the trail. "Let me see. I can't see over you guys," he cried, itching to be the first one to figure out what the round balls were that stopped every now and then only to turn and go the other way.

"No, you're too small. 'You're one slice short of a loaf of bread, and we are the rest of the loaf' is what Dad used to say. You know, like a cow with one less teat for milking." Beth giggled.

"Yeah, but he also said it doesn't mean you can't milk that cow, you still get milk," he proudly said, meaning he can be just as much a part of things as them.

'Well, I'm sorry that I have to keep you tethered, but Mom and Dad put me in charge of your safety, so you—" Just then, one of the round figures ceased to move and made an earsplitting noise!

"Quick, bury Arthur so it doesn't see him. I think it sees us!" panicked Esther.

When they looked back, Arthur was missing. He was launched from an opening in the snow that sent him sliding in deeper. The three girls jammed their heads in at the same time to see him trying to look further into the hole.

"Look, it's a snow fort," he yelled to them.

In that moment, an older boy who had secretly moved up on them said, "Hey, what are you doing?"

The girls jumped in their skin, almost falling into each other. "We came to see what those floating things are by the bulrushes," said Voris, standing her ground.

"Hahaha. Those are heads, our heads. We are skating in the ditches of frozen water. You know, trenches for drainage," he related.

"And this hole?" demanded Voris.

"It's one of many tunnels we have. They're channeled into each other in case there's a cave in somewhere. What did you think our heads were?" he asked, with dark smiling eyes.

"We weren't sure, maybe deer or coyotes trying to see over the bulrushes," implied Beth.

"You girls can join us if you want, or do you have skates?" he asked.

"We might," piped up Voris.

In that moment, they heard Mother calling for them with her whistle. That meant it was either time to eat or time to check in due to an empty house for too long. Margaret kept track of all kids. Her ears and eyes always worked in union.

Someone grabbed Arthur and pulled him from the tunnel before he lost himself in the alluring mystery of where they snaked to. That would be an adventure for another time.

"Come in and help me with the Sunday school papers," said Mom once they were inside. The living room floor was the only place large enough to sort the Sunday school material for the kids and adult classes. They formed a sitting assembly line, passing paper after paper until they had small stacks arranged in perfect order. Afterward, they had their Saturday lunch leftovers, which meant they could each choose a leftover to eat from the last few days. Later, she had one of them set an extra supper plate seeing as she made food stretch far enough in case a visitor came. It was a common event since they were the go-to crisis home. They came hungry but never left that way. Family devotions took place every day after supper. Margaret warmed their home with her sincere character and moral qualities.

The adventurous day outside welcomed bedtime for Arthur and Esther as they sat etching frosty designs on the single windowpanes.

They resembled tree roots and branches. As Margaret watched, she thought of how God engrafted the Gentile onto the tree, making them a partaker of salvation.

> And if some of the branches were broken off, and you, being a wild olive tree, were grafted in among them, and with them became a partaker of the root and fatness of the olive tree, do not boast against the branches. But if you do boast, remember that you do not support the root, but the root supports you. You will then say, "Branches were broken off that I might be grafted in." (Romans 11:13–19)

> When they heard these things they became silent; and they glorified God, saying, "Then God has also granted to the Gentiles repentance to life." (Acts 11:18)

> "Therefore, let it be known to you that the salvation of God has been sent to the Gentiles, and they will hear it." (Acts 28:25–28)

That night, she rested on the power of God's mercy for all those who wanted to be in His family.

The rising sun spilled over the kids' blankets, slightly warming them before they woke up. Two bedrooms were upstairs for the three older girls with two beds in each room. Arthur had his own room downstairs which was his protection from flying hairbrushes and noisy mornings.

It's Sunday morning with only a few more weeks until Christmas. Margaret woke everyone with the smell of breakfast cooking. She gathered the Sunday school papers for church and the ones for the following week, then dressed Becky and herself. Last, she set the table while Garth held their growing baby.

The girls, like Margaret when she was a girl, kicked their blankets into the air, crash-landing them onto each other's bed. Sometimes they clashed and went nowhere but straight down in a pile on the floor. One of the girls on a bunk bed in a room of her own had nowhere to kick hers except to the foot end. Not much fun in that, but sometimes it's nice to have your own room.

Arthur made his way to the kitchen before the others. Pancakes like Margaret used to make back home sat on the hot plate while more were cooking. By this time, she turned around to see her children fitted onto their chairs with forks mounted in their hands. Dad said grace, and breakfast began with Arthur jabbing the first pancake with one hand and tipping the syrup bottle in the other. It reminded Margaret of her brother George. She missed both him and Harriet.

"Is everyone ready to walk over to the church?" Dad busted out in a joyful voice. Becky was the first one to let out a positive squeal, and everyone laughed at the sound of her teeny voice coming out her tiny face with a piece of pancake clung to her two front teeth. Arthur swatted at the hanging pancake, and it flung onto Esther's plate. She didn't see where it landed, and he didn't tell her.

After church commenced with Christmas carols, a message of hope spread throughout the congregation, lighting up young faces, old faces, new faces, and all hearts. Many were reliving the hope within them like Simeon's hope was fulfilled, for his eyes beheld the Savior (Luke 2:29–32).

The children's play rolled out the steps of Jesus's birth using a real baby, making the play look authentic. It ended with clapping and the Sunday school teachers letting the kids run for the clothing tables. Every year their supporting churches sent lightly used clothing. The kids loved searching through the piles, hoping to see a fancy dress or skirt and blouse. The boys wanted jeans and warm mitts. Margaret found skates for the kids in their sizes. The girls were in a state of disbelief considering they were recently invited to skate on the icy trenches, without skates! It was a marvelous day indeed, like Christmas leading up to the real Christmas.

With the holidays beginning and school ending for a couple weeks, the girls swung their skates over their shoulders and headed for the frozen trenches to meet the others already coasting back and forth on their skates. Arthur had to be skated up ahead of time because it was easier in the house than in the snow. Sometimes his free will was spoken for in order to have situations run smoothly. They plunked him on the toboggan and wondered if it would fit down the narrow path. If not, it would display sled marks trailing down the sides and be no worse off of a narrow beaten trail that it was.

Since the past week of continual snowfall, several of the tunnels had cave-ins which would be rebuilt over the holidays. It was safely done by digging two and sometimes four ends at once with an opening on the side walls every so often, eventually allowing the older builders to meet up in the middle. This type of trick was also useful as a hunting strategy, out of sight, out of mind! *It takes cleverness to be like our sisters and brothers!*

The Savior's birthday was a couple days away, and Beth wanted to give something to Jesus. "Mom, what can I give Jesus seeing as its His birthday soon?" she asked.

"Give Him your best, and give Him your time in reading your Bible. He wants you for His birthday," vouched Margaret.

"Can you imagine how many have been saved on Christmas day?" said Dad. We mostly hear about those who have a hard Christmas."

"Christmas is hard for me," claimed a little boy sitting next to Arthur.

"Yeah, for me too. I have no one to give me anything, never mind Christmas gifts," murmured an older boy.

"Well, you're getting something this year," promised Margaret.

"I'll be happy if Jesus gives me a big meal with desert," said a hopeful ten-year-old girl.

"Yes, food is a gift from God. He never stops giving, even on Christmas," agreed Margaret.

"Okay, we better have prayer and finish our snacks before bed. It's getting late," decided Garth.

The next forty-eight hours proved to be a building up of excitement for all the kids. Margaret's family was a part of setting up tables at church for the Christmas meal. There were more people than plates, and so the girls had to wash them repeatedly for each seating. Since Esther was too short to reach, she scooped up a stool to manage the drying. Afterward, they received a bag of candy for their efforts.

Supporting churches sent candy and mittens for wrapping as gifts. Evidently, it's no mystery that kids are hard on mitts whether they lose track of one or both, leaving a possible opportunity for a pet to make a bed. It's remarkable to see a large dog trying to curl up on one mitten or a sock and somehow find it efficient enough for warmth and comfort. This always made Margaret smile.

The Christmas program also gave candy. The Sunday School teachers gave hats, more mittens, crafts, crayons, combs, bookmarks, and cross-stitch kits. Arthur and the girls created artful cards at home to give each other and Mom and Dad, along with a little homemade gift. Christmas baking was one big gift of joy to make and to eat. It appeared too that no matter what, the kids in crisis had moments of festive feelings and hearts that glorified the Lord through Sunday school, the Christmas play, and the festivities.

Margaret gave a special message of hope from her rocking chair on Christmas Eve. All were excited to hear about how God's perfect plan filled the world with hope in a new baby boy. The older kids staying with them wanted to know the rest of the story. It's natural to elaborate on Jesus's whole life even at Christmas because older ones like to understand it as a whole and not in part, for though Jesus mentioned His birth, He was about to willingly go to the cross for us. "For this cause I was born, and for this cause I have come into the world, that I should bear witness to the truth. Everyone who is of the truth hears My voice" (John 18:37). Psalm 19 covers the works and Word of God that describes her mindset and heart toward all ages, as she ministered relentlessly in and out of her rocker.

They both understood well that preaching "story style" was most effective because like many others, aboriginal people love to hear sermons in story form that include illustrations. They also enjoyed hearing Garth's messages outside preached from tree stumps, picnic tables, and a boat! "Then He got into one of the boats, which was Simon's and asked him to put out a little from the land. And He sat down and taught the multitudes from the boat" (Luke 5:3).

Managing the crisis home always included evening Bible study and prayer. The stories brought up a lot of questions that arose from Scripture. That's when the popcorn came out, and they knew it was going to be a fascinating Bible story. Garth told of the great wonders and works of God while Margaret rocked a small child, or two at once. She had infants and small children staying with them again this Christmas who experienced the peacefulness of that rocking chair and their spiritual mother in it.

As buttered popcorn aromatized the dim-lit home, their kids with the other children sat cross-legged in front of the rocking chair with eyes glued to Pastor Dad, the storyteller. Occasionally he sat and read from Margaret's chair. He was explaining the importance of listening when God tells you to do something and to not run the other way.

"Jonah learned the hard way," he began. "He resisted God's call to speak to the people of Nineveh. He was to warn them to repent before judgment came, but he chose to leave town on a ship. God brought him back by way of a whale for transportation (Jonah 1:17)."

"You mean a whale ate him," cried the younger ones.

"Yes, he was swallowed up and delivered back to town, then spewed out alive onto shore," said Garth (Jonah 2:10).

After further discussion about Jonah, he told a story of Elisha as a teaching tool in respecting others who may not have the same appearance. "And youths shouldn't call people names because something terrible can happen to them like in 2 Kings 2:23." He nodded.

"What happened in Kings?" sought Arthur.

"Well, a group of youths were calling Elisha names, then they were mauled by two bears. He was a man of God, and they mocked him by calling him baldhead. God wants us to respect the appearance of others because we're all in His image. Think on these things tonight, and tomorrow I'll tell you more about the meaning of that story. And you'll enjoy hearing about the dry bones that were erected by God!" he promised. That's when the kids glanced out the window at the cemetery, but it was already disappearing into near darkness.

Margaret cleaned up the fallen popcorn once everyone was in bed. She stood looking at her "daily altar," thinking of all the heaped-up treasures in it that took place over the years so far.

> Do not lay up for yourselves treasures on earth, where moth and rust destroy and where thieves break in and steal; but lay up for yourselves treasures in heaven, where neither moth nor rust destroys and where thieves do not break in and steal. For where your treasure is, there your heart will be also. (Matthew 6:19–21)

She looks a little older now, but as lovely as ever. On their wedding day, Garth said that her beauty was all the church needed in regards to it not being heavily decorated, and it still applied.

"In the morning before gift opening, I'll tell them the Christmas story," yawned Margaret.

"I'll help tomorrow with our dinner. Leave that big bird up to me," said Garth.

They sat in front of the decorated tree studying the different homemade gift wrapping. A small voice came from behind them. It was one of the teen girls who came to their home some time ago who wanted to express a thought. She sat between Garth and Margaret, trying to adjust her wool sweater to seal in more warmth.

"I think everyone who is born has a star light up like Jesus's star, except His is bigger. We are in His image, and perhaps our star is in the image of His star," the girl suggested.

"That's an interesting thought. I know that we are as numerous as the stars, and we will shine like the stars," replied Margaret, as she picked up her Bible from her lap to find Scriptures. "'Those who are wise shall shine like the brightness of the firmament, and those who turn many to righteousness like the stars forever and ever' (Daniel 12:3). 'Therefore from one man, and him as good as dead, were born as many as the stars of the sky in multitude innumerable as the sand which is by the seashore' (Hebrews 11:12)," she read. "It's okay to wonder about such things as long as we don't worship anything other than Jesus or add anything to the Bible."

> And take heed, lest you lift your eyes to heaven, and when you see the sun, the moon, and the stars, all the host of heaven, you feel driven to worship them and serve them, which the Lord your God has given to all the peoples under the whole heaven as a heritage. (Deuteronomy 4:19–20)

"All right, I'll just admire the splendor of all His creation. Thank you for always keeping me from looking past Him. I need to keep Him in mind with everything I study," she asserted, then picked herself up and sprinted off to bed, holding the front of her button sweater closed so no heat would escape. Garth smiled at Margaret as they both looked at the large star that topped their Christmas tree. Another day ended with gratitude toward the Lord.

CHAPTER 12

Treasures in the Altar, Life on the Edge, and 100 Hugs

The next few months brought not only Rebecca's second birthday but a turn of seasons. She still looks like a doll though. Margaret took every delightful complement she ever received about her children and gave them to God. She left no room for pride and self-accomplishment.

Beth is twelve and makes herself available when Mom needs her help. She plays with Becky, providing her with her collection of dolls that disappeared some Christmases ago, only to find them all fixed and put under the tree one Christmas morning. Beth never forgot the pleasant stinging in her heart when she unwrapped each doll to see new hair of yarn and fresh clothing.

Arthur is seven in a few weeks and already a little charmer. Last summer, he picked flowers for his mom as fast as they could spring up whether they bloomed yet or not. He's been waiting for winter to pass to go flower hunting again. Sometimes he added a frog to the hunt, becoming distracted by its desperate flip-flop hop to get to safety.

Voris is ten, and Esther is nine. They have been good helpers to Mom in taking turns with chores and watching Becky. Every week the chores would change for each of them in order to keep the cleaning a bit interesting, but no one wanted to be paired up with

Beth for dishes as a result of her losing interest and turning to a book to read. Arthur suggested they load the dishes onto the picnic table outside and let the rain take care of them; little did he know there's an old children's book about a man who put his dishes in the box of his truck and on the tailgate for the rain to clean. Evidently, they had the same idea.

Finally, winter's snow melted into spring's slush. The snow tunnels vanished, and the trenches began to support loads of frogs and toads; what two of the three states of matter can do in trenches for drainage is remarkable in that it supports life when thawed and supplies recreation when frozen! The fourth state is plasma, and although the kids are clever, they won't be super heating noble gases anytime soon; on the other hand, you never know!

The cemeteries nearby Garlow Line Baptist Church and Bethany Baptist Church were well-kept. They stood straight no matter how aged they were, but the minute something didn't look right after winter, it was repaired unlike a cemetery they had seen in their travels of old gravestones that sat crooked, half facing the sky. A few fallen ones were propped up with rocks. When evening came, all their shadows slanted in different directions leaning toward the silhouetted sky. It looked as though the two might merge as dusk slowly fell into the cemetery, and then dawn's sunrise would erase them altogether. Margaret once told the kids that these are burial grounds, not playgrounds.

With Easter at hand, a play by the kids from camp and church was about to begin. The Holy Spirit would fill it with truth and conviction. Margaret and the Sunday school teachers discussed with their group of actors and actresses beforehand how to better understand the way Jesus must have felt when He took on the sin of the world; for He knew there was no other way for us to be reconciled to God our Father and have eternity with Him unless He shed His blood for us (John 14:6). That's why He said, "It is finished," when He was about to give up His Spirit. The Lamb was provided; and He died for our past, present, and future sins (John 19:30). "Having forgiven you all trespasses, having wiped out the handwriting of requirements that was against us, which was contrary to us. And He has taken it out of the way, having nailed it to the cross" (Colossians 2:13–14).

The children who still weren't sure of their salvation, were reminded that all they had to do was accept His gift, repent with sincerity, trust in Him; and He'll save them from a Christless eternity plus remember their sins no more. "For I will be merciful to their unrighteousness, and their sins and their lawless deeds I will remember no more" (Hebrews 8:12).

Margaret would often say, "It's so easy to be saved but so hard to believe it and come to Jesus, something so simple yet is so difficult can therefore take time to become relevant to children."

The Easter Play

Events and miracles leading up to Jesus's death and resurrection that are proof of His deity.

Scene 1

On the platform in church, a canoe sat on the edge of a large blue sheet. The ends were lifted swiftly by two actors to suck and trap air underneath, then out again as it came down with force, forming what looked like waves flooding over the canoe:

"Master, Master, we are perishing!" said His disciples.

Then He arose (the actor sat up as the disciples inside rocked the canoe) and rebuked the wind and the raging of the water. And they ceased, and there was calm. But He said to them, "Where is your faith?" And they were afraid and marveled (Luke 8:24–25).

As they departed from the canoe, the sheet was draped over it and slightly tucked inside, making it look like a bed. No one in the congregation noticed that a little girl was laying in the canoe since the play began until an actor came from the ruler of the synagogue's house, saying to him, "Your daughter is dead. Do not trouble the teacher."

But when Jesus heard it, He answered him, saying, "Do not be afraid. Only believe, and she will be made well. Do not weep; she is not dead but sleeping. Little girl, arise." Then her spirit returned, and she arose immediately… The actors gave her something to eat as she emerged from the canoe (Luke 8:49–55). Smiles from the congregation spread throughout the room in recognition of that Scripture coming "alive!"

For the last miracle, groups of kids sat around the canoe, tired and starving. No one also saw the five loaves and two fish in the canoe, which was now being used as a big basket. Then He took the five loaves and the two fish, and looking up to heaven, He blessed and broke them, and gave them to the disciples to set before the multitude (Luke 9:16) The kids pretended to eat, then held their bellies with satisfaction, making the congregation chuckle. Jesus foretells His death, then dies.

Scene 2

The canoe is stood up to be used as a tomb, then secured in one corner of the play. Borrowed plants were put out for a garden scene in the opposite corner.

One of the teen boys acting as Jesus, knelt, slightly bent over a papier-mâché rock, praying in the garden of Gethsemane (Luke 22:41–71 with chapter 23 and 24 to follow), and He knelt down and prayed, saying, "Father, if it is Your will, take this cup away from Me; nevertheless, not My will, but Yours be done."

Just then, a group of teen soldiers outfitted with fake swords and breastplates came storming into the garden scene. The sleeping disciples woke up with Jesus asking them why they were sleeping and to rise and pray lest they enter into temptation. At the same time, one of the actors called Judas drew near to Jesus to kiss Him with a kiss of betrayal. As Jesus questioned Judas about his kiss, another actor jumped up and began the motion of cutting off the ear of the high priest's servant to protect Jesus. But when he struck him, his flimsy sword bent in half; and the ear dangled, then fell. Jesus happily picked up the crafted ear to reattach it as in the biblical miracle. Laughter came from the congregation as they searched their memories for what should take place next.

After arresting Jesus, the soldiers took Him to be dealt with cruelly while the actor of Peter denied he knew Him three times (Luke 22:61). On the third denial, one of the little kids, dressed up as the rooster, crowed at him for the last time, but his powerful call fizzled out as Peter ran off to find a place to weep over what he had done. The laughable rooster jumped the "kindled fire" and darted in the same direction, suggesting he was chasing after him. It gave the congregation a quick chance to release the increasing lump in their throats before the next painful scene.

Jesus was taken back and forth from the actors of Pilate to Herod to decide on who should command His death, a death decided by Jesus and His Father before He was born, in the first place. Neither one wanted to put Him to death. The actors playing the part of the chief priests and other men, persuaded Pilate to have Him crucified.

"Crucify Him," screamed the chief priests over and over. Joining them were the others who called for the same judgment, clueless of the double fact that this is not only their Saviour but that He chose to go through with His crucifixion in order to take the sin of the world upon Himself; He was obedient unto death (Philippians 2:7–8) but made Himself of no reputation, taking the form of a bondservant and coming in the likeness of men. And being found in appearance as a man, He humbled Himself and became obedient to the point of death, even the death of the cross.

A multitude of kids and teen actors followed Jesus to Calvary. The actor, Simon, bore the cross part of the way for Jesus. "Now as they led Him away, they laid hold of a certain man, Simon a Cyrenian, who was coming from the country, and on him they laid the cross that he might bear it after Jesus" (Luke 23:26). Next, the teen soldiers held up a thick cardboard cross with railway spikes in it as Jesus stood in front of it wearing the crown of thorns. There was nothing but silence, then someone switched the lights off except for a lamp behind Him. Red food color in syrup streamed down His face, dripping onto His costume; and with His arms stretched wide, He said, "Father, forgive them, for they do not know what they do" (Luke 23:34). The part of the two criminals on their crosses was included by the reading of Scripture (Luke 23:39–43). Then Jesus, all bloody, said, "Father, into Your hands I commit My spirit" (Luke 23:46). The actresses who followed Him stood at a distance watching these things. The inscription written over Him said, "Jesus of Nazareth, the King of the Jews" (John 19:19). It was Pilate who had this written on the sign because he knew who He was.

It was the chief priests of the Jews who wanted the sign changed to say, "He said, 'I am the King of the Jews.'"

Pilate answered, "What I have written, I have written" (John 19:20–22).

The lamp was unplugged, and the scene changed to the sheet covering the front of the canoe that stood against the wall in darkness. A large papier-mâché rock was rolled in front of it. All lights came back on, and the rock suddenly rolled away to produce an empty tomb as the sheet fell. When the girl actresses came with prepared spices and fragrant oils and saw Jesus was gone, two boy actors in shining garments stood in the tomb with the girls near by and said, "He is not here but is risen" (Luke 24:1–6). Excitement funneled from the girls to the apostles. Peter ran to the tomb to find nothing, nothing but linen cloths lying by themselves (Luke 24:12).

The play ended with the rock, sheet, and cross in a pile and Jesus standing before the congregation clothed and alive!

The End

No one left that day without seeing the Holy Spirit in action through those kids and Scripture. Afterward, the teen choir put on an Easter cantata.

Picnics were well underway now that June fashioned its way in. Every kid had something to chase in the field again. Frightened snakes slithered between rocks to avoid the sneakers that had fast feet in them, blades of grass hid the low-laying toads who popped up to see what was pounding the ground so loud, and rodents in highest community order ran for the best underground security tunnels.

Once berries were out, it meant jam making would immediately begin; but canning peaches, pears, green beans, tomatoes as chili sauce, and pickled cucumbers were favorites. The most effective way in canning depended on age. The youngest (Esther and Arthur) washed the produce. The oldest (Beth and Voris) blanched, then peeled what needed peeling, and Margaret did the packing. And she, being highly thoughtful, made all the grape juice for communion, that being for two churches!

That summery Sunday morning brought in a playful mix of sun and clouds over the grassy field that was blanketed in snow not too long ago. Arthur and the girls were running through the field charging after the shadows of gliding clouds that were cast over them and the ground. But playing on a Sunday morning was infringing on preparation for church. Margaret had to regather the kids because they went in different directions trying to keep up with the moving shadows. Becky was always easy to find. Margaret just looked for the stroller that had a dressed-up cat flopped in it. One of the kids called her the Barbie doll with a Barbie cat, although the grouchy cat wasn't as cute.

People streamlined into the first church. Full capacity was common in both churches, and in between the two services, Esther's job was to hurry home after the service at Bethany Baptist Church and start a roast for supper before the p.m. service at Garlow Line Baptist Church. It seemed no one ever had a dull moment on Sundays, no time for one of those!

The sermon was on prophecy about the will of the Father. "This is the will of the Father who sent Me, that of all He has given Me I should lose nothing but should raise it up at the last day. And this is the will of Him who sent Me, that everyone who sees the Son and believes in Him may have everlasting life; and I will raise him up at the last day" (John 6:39–40). Garth gave a superb message. The young people looked relieved and more assured of their salvation. Any little nudges of fear left over broke away to let the light shine in.

About a year later (1970), when Becky was three, they moved from the parsonage at Garlow Line into a house next to Bethany Baptist Church.

By 1972, they began Faith Baptist Indian Mission which was a great blessing. As a result of the success, they merged it with Baptist Mid-Mission in 1974–1975. Baptist Mid-Missions Missionary

Apprentice Program provided several workers for camp and Vacation Bible School who later went on to full-time ministry.

In 1976, Margaret's passion for the children to learn of Christ and to be saved was as strong as ever. There were difficult times, but she always had seeds to cultivate in the hearts and minds of the those in her ministries. Her life came down to the life of others accepting the Savior because when it comes down to it, nothing is as important in life.

From their first ministry to now and beyond, the Lord enabled Garth and Margaret to win souls, disciple believers, establish churches and kids' clubs, direct camps, teach Bible Institute, and serve several times as field chairman for the Indian Ministries of Baptist Mid-Mission. Margaret was right by Garth's side. The Lord gave her ideal ways for teaching Scripture, such as a board with their questions taped to it and the answer under it for all to see. They shared the reading of chapters that she broke down along the way for the class to understand. And skits were always a fabulous way to interpret the contents of Scripture. She saw loads of miracles and baptisms, with their salvation in action sailing from one week into the next.

Arthur was fourteen and the girls were nineteen, seventeen, sixteen, and nine. By this time, they had grown up with and around several aboriginal children and adults who were nothing short of brothers and sisters in Christ. Margaret was loved for the spiritual parent she was known for. She demonstrated Scripture by the way she lived and taught, even her cooking meant "I love you" for the reason that she'd cook the very fish caught at camp by that child, for that child.

Also in 1976, the Bible Institute out of Bethany Baptist Church came into existence. Margaret marched alongside of that as well. She had all the criteria for partnering with Garth and a joint desire to please God in everything said and done.

The "treasures" God continued to give her were rocked day and night. They felt the touch of God's love through song, prayer, and stories. Infants felt the warmth and safety, sensing Jesus whom they did not know yet. Big kids had biblical stories structured in their minds, then performed as skits and plays. The good news was that it became increasingly hard to know how many were saved with kids coming and going over the years, and though God was keeping track, Margaret loved to watch the children and teens recognize Jesus as the holy One and only One to follow. She'd say, "He will lead you through your salvation. We all have our own path to walk down in life at our own pace and at the end of it will be our crowns. There are five crowns as rewards, the victor's crown, (1 Corinthians 9:25) the crown of rejoicing (1 Thessalonians 2:19), the crown of righteousness (2 Timothy 4:8), the crown of life (James 1:12, Revelation 2:10), and the crown of glory (Hebrews 2:7). Be sure your work will stand the test of fire (1 Corinthians 3:12–15), but remember, Jesus Himself is our chief reward."

Then came planning for the big mission trip to Haiti—one week to get there, one week to stay, and one to get back. Margaret found someone she knew well to stay with her kids.

"Mom, how long are you and Dad gone for?" asked Arthur.

"Don't worry, it'll be long enough to get into trouble." Beth laughed.

"Three weeks, and I need you to look after the outside duties for us," stated Mom, ignoring Beth's comment.

"Good thing I'm here to keep watch over you all," said Voris, tipping her head to one side with hands on her hips and elbows pointing outward.

"Yes, Voris, I count on you and Beth. You girls are both great caretakers. It's in your hearts to be," she went on to say.

"We will miss you all. Not sure how much we can stay in touch though," added Dad.

"Well, don't worry about us. We can fend off starvation and thunderstorms, or whatever comes our way," snickered Esther.

Becky was skirting around in her mind for something funny to say too but could only think of the tears that were about to run down her face that her brave little heart couldn't stop. Mom hugged her, letting her hide her teary face against her sweater.

Once on the plane, there was no turning back, and they flew off into the sunset.

"The evening is clouded in this part of the sky tonight," said Margaret as the brilliant sun no longer threatened to scorch their eyes. Instead, it was revealing the sculpted edges of the clouds from behind, giving them extra definition, then lighting the top ridges with a dazzling silver lining.

"We don't see the clouds streaked with silver very often." Garth marveled. "It reminds me of a wordless banner yet is saying a lot by showing the majesty of God's work," he added.

Finally, the large, full moon appeared and sat glowing in its swollen state. The starry sky stretched into the vastness with no end in sight while all the travelers slept, perhaps some trusting their night in flight to God.

Arriving at the end of an exhausting week, they left the airport in Haiti with the ride sent to bring them to the designated village. One hundred beautiful dark little faces peered in at them as they turtled their way between the crowd of kids and parents. The driver crawled through a sudden opening as individuals moved outward from the truck, wheeling his way through the thicket of people.

"This is it! This is where you stay," said the driver.

They climbed out, grabbed their luggage, and were left standing in the middle of everyone as he lunged forward with his old truck, then tiptoed until passing the end of the crowd.

"Welcome. I will show you where to go," called an English-speaking man with gleaming white teeth set perfectly in his Hollywood smile.

The following week was superb! Margaret's story time had become famous with the children. She read and held up illustrations as the interpreter followed along. There's not much more lovely in life than when you're surrounded by one hundred jubilant faces with hope growing in Christ. Each day, Jesus was praised for the Creator He is and for His nonnegotiable plan of His death and resurrection that Margaret taught in a way they could understand. On the last day, the children cried and hugged her one at a time with one hundred memorable hugs.

Years 1977–1978 was a continuation in ministry with no dull days in sight. In fact, dull days would have been welcomed seeing as everyone was about to lose their lives! There are strongholds in the world of ministry that can only be broken by prayer and Christ, and then there are times when something happens out of the blue, and you know evil is trying to get a grip every moment it can through an incident that arises. They thanked their heavenly Father, their Savior, and His Holy Spirit for always moving at the required speed under all circumstances when a thorough prayer may not be possible. God doesn't have to wait for us to ask for help, for He's not limited by prayer or time.

The Roberts family was Arizona bound to meet a missionary and pick up her U-Haul to take to Salamanca, New York. They left their home in Six Nations, Brantford, Ontario, to drive across the states to Winslow, Arizona, where she was located. Once they left from there, their missionary friend drove on ahead to Salamanca at her own pace while Margaret and family made a camping trip out of their travels. Nights were especially eye-opening as far as making sure poisonous creatures weren't crawling in the kids' blankets before they were to crawl in themselves. Parents on the outside and everyone in-between was the old strategy, but the kids are now old enough to tent it without Mom and Dad. The van was the new tent for the parents; however, they parked close to the kids in case predators came snooping during the night. Of course, animals often gave themselves away due to the moonlight displaying their larger-than-life shadows scurrying by. Beth, Voris, and Esther had a tent together with Becky tucked in the center; and it wasn't believed that any prowling animal could get near three teen girls and survive, not since living in camp life!

"We need to read, then pray," Mom began to say as her, and Garth approached them in one of the tents.

"Yes, let's gather together for prayer before its dark." Dad motioned, swinging his hand into the air for Arthur to come.

"God's gonna turn the light out pretty soon," cut in Becky.

"Well, He can turn it out 'cause I'm tired" came a dry voice from Arthur. "And I'm thirsty. I feel like a piece of driftwood."

"I can pour some water on your dry bones." Voris laughed.

"Yeah, well, God didn't need water to erect. Hey, Dad, you still didn't explain the Scripture for the dry bones," said Arthur, now perked up.

"I did a few years ago. Did you forget it now?" he asked.

"We have time for one story. Does everyone want to hear that one?" asked Mom. Five yeses rolled off five tongues, and the story began with prophecy (Ezekiel 37:1–14).

"There was a valley full of dry bones laying in the open. And Ezekiel, a priest, passed by them, all around. He looked at them and they were dryer than driftwood," Dad said, adding to Arthur's drab condition. "God asked him if these dry bones could live! Ezekiel said, 'Oh, Lord God, You know.'"

"So God had him prophesy to the bones to hear the Word of the Lord by saying, 'Surely, I will cause breath to enter into you and you shall live,'" added Mom, pretending to be Ezekiel with a commanding voice. "All of a sudden, the noise of rattling bones filled Ezekiel's head, rattling against his brain for it was a great slain army that was individually joined bone to bone, at once! Then sinews and flesh grabbed onto their bare bones, and skin covered them. But something was wrong. They just laid there without any response; not one was breathing."

"Yes, but then up from the ground, they stood when breath entered them by command. They lived and stood on their feet!" finished Dad.

"God gave back their lives and army power again?" asked Arthur.

"Well, God spoke it and performed it whereas it's not mentioned what that army did from there," acknowledged Dad.

Margaret explained the conjoined meaning of that true story as Israel being the dry bones since they lost hope and were cut off from God. "But they will know the Lord is the Lord because He'll open their hearts. He'll put His Spirit in them, for they're spiritually dead. Therefore, they will be born from above under the new covenant," she interpreted.

Now as the natural light went out and sleep prevailed, no one could have known that the possible danger in the night was just a precursor of the day ahead for Margaret's family. It would have been better to stave off an annoying creature in the night than meet the chasm that can't be chased off.

That morning the trip resumed for Salamanca, New York, until they reached the mountainous Wolf Pass at Canyon De Chelly. Mountains stood all around that were not only beautiful but somewhat intimidating in that they seemed close enough to swallow the road and everyone on it.

"It beats me how the large vehicles have enough brakes to handle passes such as this one," Margaret said out loud after a stretch of quietness.

"They need to judge their position versus curvature and slopes in the road. They can't miss any signs either. It's a constant estimation of distance and elevation," explained Garth.

"You mean like the time your log truck tore over that bridge down the mountainside?" asked Arthur.

"Yes, except that road and bridge wasn't paved or maintained. The truck got away on me as a result of it. And although this road is good, there's still no guarantee," he ended saying, when their van and U-Haul suddenly came to a halt!

"What's wrong?" asked Margaret, putting her book down to observe her surroundings. At the same time, everyone looked out their windows to see if there was a problem.

"Garth, I think we're going backward. And what's that noise I'm hearing?" she said, with wide open eyes.

"Uh, it's the sound of gravel. We are on the shoulder, and it's too soft to let us out," he said with reluctance.

They all sat in disbelief of the implications of the situation. The gravel was crunching as they moved closer to the thousand-foot drop into the canyon! The looming sounds of gravel and heavy breathing from nostrils amalgamated, becoming louder in their heads. The level of discomfort tipped the scales, and they could see each other's screaming eyes searching for a way to eject their bodies out of the van but were too numb to go through with it. Margaret couldn't get out. It wasn't possible without enough ground for her to step on to! It was like looking out of a small plane, so she drew her eyes to the roadside that was visible. While she turned, she saw Garth praying and bowed her head to God.

A knock rattled against their windshield with a construction worker standing before them, hook in hand. He grabbed for the van's tow hook and connected his hook, shackling them together with a clanging sound loud enough to drown out the crushing gravel. He was in a hurry and wasn't worried about gracefulness. Running to his open truck door, he shot himself up into the seat, stabbing the clutch with one foot and the accelerator with the other, careful not to let the van or U-Haul turn more outward from the back end toward the cliff of the canyon. The nameless man hauled them up and over the unforgiving hill.

Once on top, Margaret surveyed the area one last time, then glanced at her wedding ring and kids. Clearly this was not a dull and relaxing day that everyone craved for in between packing and unpacking and putting tents up and down every day, no time for one of those! But they did love the silence once the mixed noises died out. Naturally, gratitude was expressed to the man who ceased the moment to take on a serious situation, and God received the glory.

The rest of the trip to New York had nothing much to reveal until they arrived in Chicago. Margaret was driving, and unfortunately the standard shifter became stuck between first and second gear. The bustling traffic was heavy, and Garth woke up to blaring horns and crunching gears. But Margaret pushed on through the rush hour saying, "I'm going to do this!" And she did. Margaret's last words that day were "Well, the way I see it, trips aren't supposed to be boring. God was with us and knew the outcome all along."

CHAPTER 13

Ministry Continued, Margaret's Departure

> Go therefore and make disciples of all nations, baptizing them in the name of the Father and of the Son and of the Holy Spirit, teaching them to observe all things that I have commanded you; and lo, I am with you always, even to the end of the age. (Matthew 28:19–20)

Every missionary who believes in Jesus Christ believes in the Great Commission! According to the Lord, Garth and Margaret were to leave behind their existing mission field and allocate to Kenora, Ontario, to minister to the Ojibway people. Kenora is located at the north end of Lake of the Woods, and their outreach was to the Kenora District, which extended from the northern border of Minnesota to the subarctic and is bordered on the west by Manitoba. This included girls' and boys' summer and winter camp at Camp Bemahdezewin (VBS), Bible Seekers Club in Kenora, as well as in Minaki (a village thirty-five miles North of Kenora), jail ministry, Bible study, teaching out of the Bible Institute, and the beginning of Berean Baptist Church.

Their grown kids were gone to Bible college while Rebecca was nearing teen hood. The news of moving was a blow to her on account of her whole life consisting of the two churches of Bethany Baptist and Garlow Line Baptist, as well as Camp Owendi. Margaret shared the same affection as her daughter for all the friends and home they would leave behind. It was terribly difficult with the added distance between her and her siblings, making for a mountain of comfort in demand at times like this. However, she did feel some excitement for the new ministry with Mom and Dad! Her resilience was shaped by a healthy relationship with God and her parents.

It took some time to settle into their new life in Kenora; nevertheless, the Ojibway people were amiable and family oriented. Margaret would soon come to appreciate the fact that the Ojibway people, like the Seneca people, are warm and loving. However, they had a big advantage since Garth made two visits there the year before they moved to see what the needs were in Kenora.

They bought a parcel of land and a double-wide trailer, which was quite different from what they were usually living in; however it lacked nothing in terms of common comfort and adequate space. With Margaret's adult children in Bible college, they used the extra space for children in crisis. The rocking chair had a new home but same job.

It all began with outreach ministries developed with the three Kenora area reserves of the Dalles Reserve, the Rat Portage Indian Reserve, and the Washagamis Bay Reserve. There they established Bible clubs, having around thirty children, fifteen teens, and twelve adults to start with. They were often averaging sixty. Vans were full of kids who spilled out upon arrival for activities and food. Margaret's record in the past of keeping up with flipping burgers, stuffing hot-dog buns, swatting bugs away yet keeping an eye on the active children, was indeed sharp as ever. She was a responsible servant who never closed her eyes until the day was done.

December was coming, and the Christmas program was in order; that's one of the best parts of the season! It would be their first Christmas club at Washagamis Bay Reserve, and judging by how great their past experiences were with clubs, they knew this would follow suit. Margaret's missionary friend, Ruth, was a great blessing to their ministry. She joined in the work and the fun. "Let me lift those refreshments into the van, Margaret," said Ruth, reaching for the box.

"Yes, thank you. Think all this party food will fit in here?" asked Margaret.

"If not, it'll fit fine in the bus with Garth as long as he doesn't have an overload of kids to pick up. He looks like Santa in that seventy-two-passenger bus. It's even painted red and white" Ruth laughed.

"And I feel like Mrs. Claus with all these Christmas gifts for the kids," added Margaret.

"I guess that makes me Santa's helper, or Mrs. Clause's at this point." Ruth giggled.

"Ho ho ho, I'm ready to go," sang Garth. "I got the little reindeer in the bus, hun." He paused, referring to Becky.

"Okay, we'll meet you there. I'm thinking Ruth and I will be unloaded and set up by the time you arrive with more reindeer." She smiled smartly.

It turned out to be eighty-five kids, some parents, and just enough gifts and food for everyone. Several children and one mother accepted the Lord that godly day of festivities.

That night, Mr. and Mrs. Clause kindled the idea of starting a church. That hope began smoldering before it caught fire over a year later when a missionary team of men and women with Garth and Margaret planted Berean Baptist Church for the people of Kenora and surrounding area. All those kids and parents were just one good reason to start a church!

It all began at the first collective meeting of missionaries teamed with Garth and Margaret. They named the church after Acts 17:10–12.

> Then the brethren immediately sent Paul and Silas away by night to Berea. When they arrived, they went into the synagogue of the Jews. These were more fair-minded than those in Thessalonica, in that they received the word with all readiness, and searched the Scriptures daily to find out whether these things were so. Therefore,

> many of them believed, and also not a few of the
> Greeks, prominent women as well as men.

Berean Baptist Church wasn't sizeable. It was a simple looking, straightforward, rectangular house which they rented; but what took place inside was sizable, not so simple, and totally biblical! Margaret's challenges consisted of teaching their new students in Sunday school with her prepared lessons, homemade communion preparation as throughout the prior years, and driving the Sunday school kids to church and back. That's how it is when the air you breathe is ministry. (But it wasn't until 1987 that the church became organized by writing the constitution and bylaws.)

On the agenda was another Bible club, this one being in Minaki. It was a Bible Seekers Club that brought more children to know the Lord. The village was thirty-five miles north of Kenora, but that didn't matter. For that's a part of outreach. Margaret taught Sunday School, and Garth led the singing until they could send a willing young couple who were attending Berean Baptist Church to take over that ministry.

In July of 1982, Berean Baptist Church was fuller than ever, and Camp Bemahdezewin was up and running. Becky was fifteen now and finished the tenth grade in a Christian school located in Minnesota, USA. She came home when she could throughout the year. Kids from the area and beyond joined in the summer frolic. Fishing, swimming, and games may have made up most of the physical part of camp fun; but the Christian material, including learning biblical fundamentals, plus following dialogue for skits and plays, were the spiritual aspects of fun. Being a winter camp as well, it added to the outdoor activities much like how Camp Owendi was.

With help from Ruth, they opened a drop-in center in town which grew equally fast. Sincere ministering was the reason for that. Regular visitation and counseling took place to minister to people who were broken.

Moreover, Margaret made regular visits to the jail for women and teen girls. The challenge was huge but wonderful! As painful as it was for these equal creations of God to be incarcerated, Margaret told them if anyone knows how to love them, it's the God who made them. Once they accepted that, a relationship slowly developed into trust, then repentance. Sometimes it was the other way around.

She was known to bring some of these women home when they were released until she could get them into an apartment on assisted living. She ministered to them like a mother, and nothing shocked her. However, being surprised is different! One Christmas Eve, the hospital called her, asking if she'd bring a one-year-old home while her mother recovered from a medical condition. The next day, the mother, who had been arrested prior to her treatment, was released and spent Christmas with them, then ended up getting an apartment.

Garth pastored the men in jail, which was no less difficult. There was a common ground of issues that the men and women had, often being either neglect while growing up, abuse of sorts, or a broken spirit for far too long that lead to a drug of choice. Either way or either one, God stood on both sides of the bars, giving words to Garth and Margaret and forgiveness to His children who asked. She told them, "Our Mediator is omnipresent and limitless."

Becky had been attending camp for the summer since her completion of grade ten but would be leaving again. Margaret was missing her youngest daughter already, knowing she'd have to accept letting go of her soon. That week, they left the staff in charge of camp while they made a supply run and planned for the drive to bring Becky back to Minnesota.

"Are you ready to go, Garth? I'll be done here right away. I'll be glad to get a few things from town for the camp, such as more blankets, now that it is getting cooler out and just to be at our other home for a change," said Margaret.

"I'm glad you still consider camp one of your homes. Want me to carry something to the vehicle for you?" he inquired.

"No, I'm not taking much, just our clothes to wash," she said as she lunged forward to plant her basket onto the seat. "Don't forget Princess though. She needs a break too." Margaret laughed.

"Yeah, going home gives her some time with us before coming back out and maybe some time for us to see each other over dinner," he hinted.

"I want to go home too though it won't be for long," chimed in Becky. "Minnesota will be expecting me for school, but I loved being with all the kids and staff again."

"Yes, my dear, you are a good friend to the others. You may not know it, but you're a big help to us. You spice up the gloomy days when me and Dad aren't so energetic." Margaret smiled.

Becky did well while her siblings continued in different Bible colleges away from home. Early on, she realized they weren't seeing one another either, and if they're doing okay, so can she! Mom and Dad were just happy to have her at home. Plus, it made it a little easier because they missed the others; having one is better than none. The drive back would be nine hours one way, but a quality nine hours with Becky.

Once they left her and returned home, the next couple of days would bring them to the stores again to buy the rest of the camp supplies and enjoy the faces around town. Of course, Garth found opportunities to mini preach to those he crossed paths with. Margaret spoke about camp with mothers who had kids with them. What a team they built since she met "the new face" in church, and he met the "one he thought was too lovely to have!"

That week back went interestingly well. Not only did they have a canoe trip planned for the teen boys; but a large boat with a windshield, railings, trailer, and motor was provided, which meant more water sports!

Another highlight was the two Mt. Everest climbers who brought their tents from their monumental climb and donated them to the kids' camp with a great story attached. The kids helped to set them up, then grabbed a snack, and spot on the ground or bench to listen.

"God was on that mountain!" one of the men proclaimed, as they sat around the fire. "He caught me more times than I want to count from falling into the nothingness. Only the clouds were our witness to the near tragedies that sat above and below. There were times I dared not cry for the reason that I would not have been able to see my footing through icy eyes. And you have to be a very patient person seeing as you never knew what your next step might exactly look like until you took it," he said, with a dramatized voice like that of an actor.

"And when the wind starts to blow and your blood feels like its curdling from the cold, you have to remind yourself why you're hanging from a rock," said the other climber.

"Why did you want to climb and hang from that mountain?" asked one of the kids.

"Because then we can tell others that God is obviously bigger than Mt. Everest if we can climb it. Most people wouldn't attempt a mountain being higher than the Tower of Babel, and though we weren't trying to reach God like those in the Bible were, we climbed it knowing God, the rock, is within us. 'Lead me to the rock that is higher than I' (Psalm 61:2)," they said.

"Well, God is our rock to hang onto," stated Margaret. With that said, everyone acknowledged Him as the highest.

From that night on, the boy's camp, then girl's camp, took turns sleeping a few at a time in the new bright orange tents imagining the crooked terrain going up into the clouds that these tents were a part of. One night a salad of words was thoughtfully shared among each other as to how they would react to Mount Everest's conditions. "How great is the wind that makes my footing unsteady," surged a howling voice from one girl.

"How deep the darkness that swallows my last hope of morning ever coming for me," bellowed a second girl.

"How vast the space should I fall into it in flight to the ground!" whispered a third. A moment of silence gripped the girls, then unlocked their fearful thoughts into how sovereign God was by keeping those climbers safe.

Other ministries had been rolling along such as the Bible Institute out of Baptist Mid-Missions that Garth was teaching. Margaret was very much a part of it for what would later add up to be thirty-five years in total. Her service was from a servant's heart, and she was gracious every year of the way for those years of her life. There wasn't a thing you couldn't talk to her about. She was never judgmental, never talked about others unless it was positive, never loved one more than the other, always went to her husband for spiritual and scriptural answers when needed, "And if they want to learn something, let them ask their own husbands at home" (1 Corinthians 14:35). She was serious and for real. Other women who came to Christ, some already believers, began studies with them out of the institute and later went on to a ministry of their own after graduating with either a Bible diploma or a Christian worker's certificate or both. Others came for Bible study each week at the church. Some were couples, some were single, but all were willing to put God first in their lives.

Then there was marriage counseling, a priority for those who decided to step into the life of marriage. Both Garth and Margaret enjoyed looking back at their courting days, revealing the steps they took in getting to the altar. The young couples loved when Margaret told her story about her ring in the mail, the gown on the mannequin, and her Bible bouquet, a wedding that had several different dates up until a final one which mostly took place through letters and his grandmother's phone.

Some months later, plans for a better outdoor kitchen at Camp Bemahdezewin was drawn up. Twice the bears had helped themselves to Margaret's cookware hanging atop the prep table and broke standing structures that just couldn't be resurrected a third time. They wait at the top of the big hill that exits the camp until everyone goes home for a while before they dismantle the place. She said she just wanted a kitchen to function, not perfection. She knew the bears would find another opportune time. Friends from Six Nations came to help with what turned into multiple building projects. Plus, some ladies came to counsel at the girl's camp.

Dishes continued to be washed outside with more table room to work with and eating took place on new picnic tables, plus extra benches to sit on. It was roughing it by no exaggeration; however, roughing it just got better! The same critters who fought for a piece of the action during meals now had more places to hide and wait for kids to drop morsels.

All that night, Princess weaved between the tents to the bottom of the hill and back again, taking naps only until the morning light crested the hill of interest. She was a suspicious dog for a good reason.

For the next five, six years (1988–1993), good things continued in the house of the Lord, bringing people back to church every
Sunday. Plays based on the life of Jesus, music to restore hearts to
peacefulness, and God's Word to restore people with various problems all had their share.

In Sunday school, Margaret continued to show the kids, not
just tell them, about their Savior. They drew pictures to hang up,
made sheep to express their position in Christ, and recited effective
Scripture aimed at assurance of their salvation in a way they could
understand; sometimes acting out Scripture was possible. They sang
songs of salvation belonging to our God and songs of unity with God
and, of course, the song "Jesus Loves Me" and so many more.

As far as camp went, it was time to improve the outdoor kitchen
again with the addition of a hot water tank and a designated washup
area. New sleeping accommodations were built in cabin style, and
outdoor restrooms that completed their camp buildings. Outdoor
events in between it all, such as canoeing, boating, and fishing, were
breaks from the work. Margaret championed the outdoors with her
experience and talents. She matched the rugged outdoors through
each season with her ability to adjust in all situations and weather
conditions. She always loved to investigate God's gifts of seasons and
explain the process of the cycle of life. A good analogy of hers was
the colorful season of autumn, when life departs the plants and their
seeds hit the ground. It reflects our resurrection, "What you sow is
not made alive unless it dies" (1 Corinthians 15:36).

The earlier years of ministry seemed to go from a gradual
speed to zipping along exponentially. (1993–1997). In 1993, Camp
Bemahdezewin's kitchen was again improved, this time as an indoor
building! The proposal went in, and an agreement came out. Men
and women got together to make it happen! Margaret and staff had
countertops, a sink, two commercial stoves, and storage shelves. Fires
were mostly for campfires now. The kitchen was a good plan, but the
wild animals didn't think so.

New staff joined the current staff, one of them being Carrie
Thompson. Like the others, she was a blessing to both Garth and
Margaret, which would result in a lifelong friendship. She was a part

of building the new kitchen, plus had an extensive ministry in heading up Junior Church, teaching Sunday school and Bible club, plus a ministry with young offenders. Her Bible degree was a great asset, as well as her music degrees. She played multiple instruments and often played one for the Sunday service and for the kids' ministries.

With extended plans, they built an outdoor dining room and chapel. However, Garth still preached at times from a boat or a pulpit by the lake. It was the same spot he taught morning Bible study if it was nice out.

One stormy summer night, Princess, the on call camp dog, made her way to the foot of the hill at camp and laid motionless. It was as though she didn't notice the turbulence around her. The storm was without rain, and the piney forest dropped many cones and branches that would later make snow homes and food for small animals. The wind raced through the forest, trying to catch the critters in hiding, but they were champions at tunneling beneath the underbrush. Princess's sleepy head was teetering until she caught a familiar foul smell that clouded the air at the top of the hill for the past week. Suddenly her eyes went from slits to saucers, and when she stood up, so did her fur! She knew that sour odor could only belong to the big ugly daunting bear that has been circling the area lately, blending into the blackness of night. During the day, the kids had their fun; and long after evening, he wanted his. He stood in predominance, for he was the largest and most powerful bear in the entire area. It took until the end of the week for him to inch his way closer to Margaret's new kitchen and to the sleeping kids, but the dog made the "trouble on the hill" known by blowing his cover every night. Garth had been speaking with conservation officers about the matter, which brought surveillance and a bear trap, yet they never caught him. He was out there, somewhere.

When Sunday came, Garth preached a message in church on devotion to Christ while Margaret taught her Sunday school class some important reasons for believing in Jesus. Later that day, they drove back to camp with their supplies to set up for another week of life in the outdoors. At least cooking was made easier now that she had two stoves in the new kitchen, but nothing could have prepared anyone for the shock awaiting them.

They rolled down the hill to the camp and came to a sudden stop. Something didn't feel right. Something didn't look right as they stepped out of the vehicle.

"Oh no…the kitchen. What did that monster do? He wrecked it," she angrily answered herself. "Look at the flour everywhere. It's… it's even on the ceiling. What bear reaches a ceiling?"

"Um, I think it's the big ugly one," said Garth, swiping his hair back with his hand while guessing at the height of the bear.

"And look, he peeled the protective boards over the window like an orange. The wood is damaged, and the screen nearly ripped clean off. I'd like to know why he never bothered this much with the outdoor kitchen. The more shelves you put up, the more to bring down. The bigger the kitchen, the bigger the damage. I think he just wanted to make me mad," she said with no reverence for the bear.

"I guess I shouldn't have left anything worthy in here when we left for town," admitted Garth. "I thought that nasty brute was gone now."

Meanwhile, Princess was scoping out the camp for any trace of the bear. It seemed her hair was constantly on end.

They tried to end that day on a memorable note and sat like they used to, watching the stars crowd in the sky like tiny crystal balls, waiting for one to race out of control across the curtain of darkness.

In the morning, they began the task of fixing what the bear wrecked. "I think we need to take a trip after this next round of camping just to refresh ourselves," said Margaret as they picked up the mess.

"All right. Can't disagree with that. We know we always come back in full swing after a holiday," he said.

The next day, Garth surprised Margaret with a map. "What's this for?" inquired Margaret.

"Look at what's circled on it," he said.

"Well, it says Route 35 to Louisiana. Oh, our trip! When do we leave?" she asked.

"After the camp kids go home, then two days after that, just enough time to plan what to take and pack it," he said.

Before leaving, they tied up all loose ends by organizing staff workers to replace them at camp and someone to preach for two Sundays at Berean Baptist. Princess continued to occupy the bottom of the hill after they left, sniffing for clues of what might be lurking her way.

The roads for traveling became icy topped with snow the closer they got to their destination. Once there, they rented a cabin, something like what Margaret thought they might stay in for their honeymoon but ended up staying in a quaint motel in Green Gables, New Milford, Pennsylvania.

"One thousand and three hundred miles later, and we get snow," said Margaret.

"Well let's get our stuff, get in our palace, and get dinner before we get more snow." Garth chuckled.

"When did you get so funny?" Margaret smiled.

"When did I get you?" he asked as he put his arm around her to walk with her into the cabin.

After dinner, the plan was to ride the river boat down the Mississippi River, but the streets were blocked when they stepped out of the restaurant due to the Mardi Gras parade. Who could reveal what unknown trouble might be there that a pastor and wife could walk into? Neither one of them knew what kind of parade was unfolding in the streets until they saw the strange masks and clothing, some people practically without clothing.

"I'd say it's a bit cold out to be hardly dressed," said Margaret, looking away from the people less dressed than others.

"I think we should turn around and head back before we get too far into this commotion. Don't let go of my hand," Garth said as he led her around and through the flailing arms. A crowd of masked dancers swirled toward them, swallowing them for an eerie moment, then swirled off again. Two gladiators struck each other with fake swords as they continued to fight behind a moving float truck carrying people with fancy headdresses. Margaret took a second look at how odd it appeared, to have gladiators mixed in with the glitzy floats.

"Do you know the way back to the cabin?" asked Margaret.

Just then, a dragon headdress with a set of human feet sticking out bumped into Garth but missed Margaret. The incident set off a string of events starting with his pocketed cell phone calling their second oldest daughter, Voris, in Pennsylvania. The sounds of screaming voices mixed with roaring ones on their end was alarming on her end, and if that wasn't enough, she heard gunshots ring out. She called her siblings to see the whereabouts of Mom and Dad. No one knew exactly at this point, except that they drove to Louisiana. Everyone agreed for Voris to call the police and report Mom and Dad as being in trouble, or possibly missing. The police listened to the recorded message of screams and shots and decided to look for them. Meanwhile, they made their way back to the cabin, turned the phone off before looking at it, then called it a night.

That morning, they got up and had prayer as always. Not very often was it that they needed to thank Jesus for redirecting bullets, redirecting other things maybe, but not that. Garth then turned the phone on and got ready to go out to begin a day of relaxing possibilities. But a moment later, the phone rang.

"Hello," answered Garth.

"This is the police. Is this Mr. Roberts?" asked a deep, solid voice.

"This is he. Is something wrong?"

"Yes, you and your wife were missing according to your daughter, Voris. Can you call her and tell her you're both fine? We got a call after your phone called hers with screaming on your end," he explained.

"That must have been the noise from the parade. Someone was shooting as well. Thank you, I will call her," said Garth.

"Yes, we looked into that too. Very well. Goodbye," said the officer.

Margaret wasn't sure if she wanted to step out the door since it had been so reckless out there. After all, it was a rough neighborhood, and they already had an involvement with the police. "Is this a holiday or a call-it-a-day-and-stay-in day?" She laughed. "We still can't do the river boat ride, and we can't just sit in here."

"We have a few more days here. Do you want to go to Mississippi early to visit your brother and his wife?" he asked.

"I suppose we should go today. It's early enough for the five-hour drive," replied Margaret, then called her brother to let him know.

The rest of the holiday consisted of visiting George and his wife, then their oldest daughter, Beth, and husband Dennis in Winston, Salem. They shared stories of when Beth was just a baby in an ark and how well the new camp kitchen came together back home after what happened to it.

It was a long ride back to Kenora; however, they were used to putting on the miles. "Here we are," said Margaret as they parked in front of their mobile home. "I'll be glad to get back to camp."

"You always miss the kids," said Garth.

"You do too. I saw you speaking with them before we left. Are you putting up that electric fence soon? That'll put the brute's fur on end instead of the dog's," she said, with a ruthless smile that made Garth laugh.

"I'll get the fence today and gather help to put it up this week," he replied.

"Sounds good," said Margaret.

The fence went up, and the kids were made aware of its power. Garth told them it's enough to send off the brute for good.

Year 1997 was another great year! More building took place, this time resulting in a large new church. They would be moving from the existing Berean Baptist Church on September first, into the new one. Inside they had an auditorium downstairs, plus multiple rooms for different classes, and God was praised for filling them with kids. Many came to build, help move, and set up. Bible Seekers Clubs had their parties there, and the Christmas program had all the room they needed for putting on their plays and skits in the upstairs auditorium.

In 1998, they had a formal church dedication with Rev. Tim Friesen as the speaker. He was a Canadian representative of Baptist

Mid-Missions, Canada. Followed by this was their fellowship dinner. Two hundred people gathered to celebrate. Many churches and contributors were recognized at this dedication by Baptist Mid-Missions. The night was filled with gratitude and prayer in recognition of God and what He was doing.

In between teaching at the camp and clubs, Margaret was still rocking children day and night for mothers who couldn't be there themselves. That's as real as ministry gets. These mothers loved their children but had much to deal with before they could resume being a mother. They trusted her, and so did their children. Child services knew they could count on her being just a phone call away. All good things crowded Margert's heart, which left no room for idleness in mind or life, for she focused on Philippians 4:8–9,

> Whatever things are true, whatever things are noble, whatever things are just, whatever things are pure, whatever things are lovely, whatever things are of good report, if there is any virtue and if there is anything praiseworthy-meditate on these things. The things which you learned and received and heard and saw in Me, these do, and the God of peace will be with you.

This same year, another ministry would begin according to requests from First Nations Baptist pastors to have a culturally sensitive, local-church-based Native Baptist Bible Institute Program and to take it to various locations. This ministry would be developed under the Native American ministry team of Baptist Mid-Missions and commissioned by Birchardville Baptist Church, the church Margaret used to attend as a young girl and was married in! This ministry became the First Nations Baptist Bible Institute and Seminars.

In 2004–2016, their next call was to continue the Bible Institute out of Baptist Mid-Missions in Thunder Bay, Ontario. They moved there from Kenora, which was another difficult move from all the children they watched grow up. Some of those children Margaret either rocked in her chair, taught in Sunday school, or counseled as teens and adults. They loved her as their spiritual mother and for her endless devotion to Jesus and to them.

Their daughters Esther and Becky living in Thunder Bay was a real blessing just to be with two of their five adult kids and have some grandchildren nearby. Arthur being in Alaska was a long trip away but enjoyed trip no doubt to see him and his wife, Angela, when they could. Their daughter, Voris, a registered nurse, followed in Mom's footsteps for her career choice. Margaret was always pleased with her children. Beth, who said, "Mom was everyone's mom, but mine first!" followed in Mom's footsteps by spending much of her time looking after children.

Although they retired in 2012, they continued teaching, for God's work is never finished and they never lost heart. "And let us not grow weary while doing good, for in due season we shall reap if we do not lose heart" (Galatians 6:9). It may have been past the idea of planting and opening another set of church doors, so they opened the door of their home to carry on with the Bible Institute and taught those whom God sent. One married couple graduated in 2016, receiving their Bible diplomas. In addition, she received a Christian worker's Certificate, and he received a pastoral diploma. Pastor David Kimball agreed to have their graduation recognized at Lakehead Baptist Church in Thunder Bay, Ontario. Since then, he serves as a deacon there, and they both continue as part of the music worship team.

Margaret thanked God for every soul brought to her over the years to minister to, the goal being to lead them toward eternity by teaching them how and why putting their faith and trust in Jesus is the reason why they were even born. "Your eyes saw my substance, being yet unformed. And in Your book they all were written, The days fashioned for me, When as yet there were none of them" (Psalm 139:16).

Similar to what Oswald Chambers said, Margaret was a Christian who truly was intimate with Jesus, who never drew attention to herself but only showed the evidence of a life where Jesus was completely in control. The bearing of fruit is always shown in

Scripture to be the visible result of an intimate relationship with Jesus Christ (John 15:1–5).

The remaining three years until 2019, they traveled to Six Nations Reserves, Kenora, Alaska, Ohio for conferences and visitation with as many of their family members in various parts of the two countries as they could.

During summer, their love for nature took them to provincial and state parks. But the big trips they saved up for and went on in the past were to the Bay of Fundy, New Brunswick, and Israel. These were anniversary trips. They reminisced about the trip to the Bay of Fundy in1996 as having the highest tides in the world and one of the most productive ecosystems. They discovered in person how God dotted the ocean floor with miraculous creatures as they walked hand in hand around the colorful characters. Margaret was in her chemistry and biology class again! Some invertebrates, such as the purple sea star, large snails and jellyfish, were left behind in the absence of the tide. Hilarious crabs with only part of their faces exposed from under the ocean floor stared at them like they were enemies, and things they weren't sure of lay looking up at them in an array of colors and shapes.

Afterward, Garth had to pull her away from the ocean platform to go for lunch. "Well, shall we go for a lobster meal?" asked Garth.

"We could have one right here! We should be able to find everything we need to make a meal, including the salad." Margaret laughed. "Hurry and snap up that seaweed for a tossed salad before the tide comes in," she said as she stood looking at it, laughing.

Margaret had a candid personality and sense of humor that made her attractive which others commented on; however, she gave every complement she ever received, including of her marriage and children to God.

But the trip of a lifetime to Jerusalem, Israel, on their fortieth anniversary in 1997 was most incredible. They recalled their footsteps in New Brunswick and in Israel. "Every step we took were in His," said Margaret, referring to everything was made by Him; therefore, He's been where they were in both places.

"Right," said Garth. "And our last step will be stepping with Him into heaven."

"Yes, and when we were in Israel, it felt pretty surreal I must say. I suppose others feel the same way once they're in that culture and walking the roads and paths that Jesus took. It was like following behind Him. I can almost see Him now," she added.

"It certainly was significant," ended Garth.

The Lord enabled Garth and Margaret to be an effective team in marriage and ministry. They enjoyed every mission in life, all the kids' camps, all the kids' clubs, all the teaching, all the praying, all the church ministry, and all the rocking. But now she was stepping into a new mission in her life. She needed to face the end of the race to reach the beginning of eternity with her Savior. First, her faith would work to secure her family's hearts in accepting her departure. Sharing Scripture with her husband was her strength. Awaiting her soon to be heavenly home with Jesus was her hope. Leaving her unwell earthly body was her freedom. Yet the part of her that lives on are her own children and everyone's memories.

The Remaining Thirty Minutes

Margaret was delicate but strong, in anticipation but ready, still in love with her husband but Jesus was waiting, sad to leave her kids, but prepared to meet her Savior and Heavenly Father. She had one small hand in her husband's in this life and the other in God's in the next; one had to let go.

She could still see the children with long flowing hair of deepest midnight with eyes to match, playing in the leaves; they loved her, they all loved her.

She's leaving behind her rocking chair but taking all the treasured memories of rocking them until someone came and got them.

"It's time now, Garth. I love you," she half whispered, then told him how much she loved him as they shared their last kiss. "We better read Scripture and pray," she calmly said. "I'm going now."

The way they started out, so shall they end, biblically. Garth read John 14:1–4,

> Let not your heart be troubled; you believe in God, believe also in Me.
>
> In My Father's house are many mansions; if it were not so, I would have told you. I go to prepare a place for you.
>
> And if I go and prepare a place for you, I will come again and receive you to Myself; that where I am, there you may be also.
>
> And where I go you know, and the way you know.

Garth prayed, asking Jesus to take her home, and he let go of her hand.

> For love is as strong as death. (Song of Solomon 8:6)

> Precious in the sight of the Lord
> Is the death of His saints. (Psalm 116:15)

Rockin' in the Spirit of Love

Their mother rocked slow, her face bowed low,
her heart engaged in prayer.
A wife who stood for all things good,
had much in life to bear.

She always tried to be the bride,
that God put at her husband's side,
and lived not for self but all the wealth
that God bestowed this lovely bride.

Knowing what the future stored,
she turned all children to the Lord.
She sang and read and rocked them to bed,
with a lasting impression of the Word.

When people came to her door,
revealing a child, sometimes more,
to which she mothered into the night,
will one day see, her reward, from the Everlasting Light.

With a God-filled heart from the start,
she never broke apart,
just kept her eyes on the Lamb
day and night.

His perfect plan and promises,
were nothing less than the best (a call to godly living),
though she not be perfect,
still… He was so forgiving.

With every baby gently rocked until they slept,
kept her up, never knowing there was no regret.

But God knew all, her tender, loving tears to fall,
which He honored…and bottled…and kept (Psalm 56:8).

S. S.

In loving memory of Margaret and her call to love, to teach, and to comfort God's children. Amen.

ABOUT THE AUTHOR

She was born in Thunder Bay, Ontario, Canada. Her saving year with our Lord Jesus Christ happened when she was seven years old. Much later in life, she received her Bible diploma and Christian worker's certificate through Baptist Mid-Missions with Pastor Garth Roberts as her teacher. She has been married for thirty-eight years to a man of aboriginal decent, and they have three adult boys. She doesn't know much about her father's side other than one of his parents was aboriginal and German and the other being German. Her mother is German and is warm toward aboriginal people which made Shelley, her two brothers, and two sisters feel loved for who they are. Shelley views everyone the way Jesus does, as equal children of God.